ALLEY RATS

Memoirs Of A Kid From the Burg

(1950s' & 1960s')

By

G.m. Staley

To my beloved readers,

I wrote down these faded memories for "The next generation." I want you, the children, to know what it was like growing up in the 20th century. I believe that it is important to know the past so that you can learn from those events. I used the monthly theme in the telling of my story because I remember in months or seasons better than I remember a certain year in time. I don't think it matters that I can't remember the year or how old I was at an exact time in my long life.

These memories are attached to the seasons rather than a random date. For example, I was born on January 3rd in 1951, but I'll still have birthday parties for the rest of my life. It's just easier for me to write about the month instead of the year. So forgive me if each month jumps around a bit. It is true that I am younger at the beginning of the book and older at the end, but that's just a coincidence.

Is this whole story true? When I was a child I thought like a child, is the answer. These are the events that I remember through the eyes and memories of a child. I changed some of the names because I couldn't get their permission at the time I published this book. I do stretch the truth and add forgotten details to make the story flow, but this is what I call to mind fifty years after the facts. Now go out there and write your own story. I wish you success and a very happy ending.

Sincerely,
Genevieve Staley

In memory of our wonderful parents

Gen and Ken.

They taught us how to live, laugh, & love.

ALLEY RATS

Chapters

Every month of the year has a lesson to teach us....

JANUARY was always a bitterly cold month.
I used to wish that I was born in June,
Like my mother,
But I was meant to have January
As my birthday month.

I grew up wild and free within the 4-mile square blocks of a yellow brick apartment building called "The Annex." The roach and mice infested building was constructed at least 70 years before I was born. Most people who lived in the Burg assumed that we lived on the wrong side of the railroad tracks that divided our tranquil town. The Alley Rats were downtown punks, and the kids across the tracks were uptown children. I grew to know and love both sides.

The Annex had four stories. My family lived on the second floor, apartment number 12. Of course, there wasn't an apartment number 13 because that would have been bad luck if a person lived in that apartment. I figured out at an early age that apartment 14 was really apartment 13.

My older brothers, Pete and Kenny, were born fifteen years before my little sister, Kathy and me. My mother's name was Genevieve, a favorite name of my Pup-Pup Ryan's. My Dad's name was Martin Kenneth, but all the boys in my family went by their middle names. So my Dad was Ken. Together my parents were called Aunt Gen and Uncle Ken. It was many years later that I discovered that they weren't really "Aunt or Uncle" to everyone we knew, that's just what most people called our parents. My Dad also had a sister named Genevieve, but she died when she was 12 years old in 1926 of some terrible kind of childhood disease.

When Mum found out she was going to have a baby at the age of 40, she was happy. My Dad was positive that I was going to be a baby girl, so he informed Mum that they would name the baby, Genevieve, after Mum and his dead sister. Mum, in fact, didn't like that name. Genevieve was hard to spell and very long to print. She wanted me to be named Jeanne Marie, a shorter name, after Mum's favorite teacher Sister Jean Marie. "A saintly name," Mum told my dad.

However, Dad declared that, "Saint Genevieve was already a saint." Besides he wanted his daughter named after the patron saint of Paris, France, his wife, and his dead sister.

Mum compromised, she replied that the only way she could ever name a child of hers, "Genevieve," was if that child was born on Saint Genevieve's day. Well, you'll never guess and what a surprise, I was born on Saint Genevieve's day! (January 3rd at 7:30 a.m., so there was no mistaking the date.) My dad was always a very religious man, and I think God just wanted Dad to know that He was on my dad's side. I was baptized Genevieve Marie, after my dad's dead sister and my mum's dead sister, but Mum always called me Jeanne.

*

Our father was a "fine furniture" salesman until that cold November evening when he slogged up our steep hill and died in the dining room of a sudden heart attack. It must have been many years before I was born, that my parents bought the green three cushioned, Chesterfield. That's what people in the 1950s' called their couch. Our sofa was big enough for six kids to jump on the cushions, and we did—jump, jump and jump. When a grown-up sat down, they sat inside the sofa. I think too much jumping had weakened the springs in that old living room Chesterfield. That sofa was our treasure chest.

My parents had many friends and more relatives. From time to time people would just dropped by and stayed for a chat or played cards. Whenever a grown-up visited our apartment, they sat in the sofa. Kathy and I loved it when they left. After we smiled and shouted our "goodbyes," we ran to the couch and threw the three cushions on the floor. Next, Kathy would step along the tattered edges of the sofa's worn lining, and I'd push my hand deep into the holes. Most of the time we found shiny pennies, but some days we'd stumble upon candy, lifesavers, gumbands, combs, Black Jack gum, nickels, and even dimes! We'd sit down on the living room rug and divide up our bounty. Kathy got the pennies, gumbands for her ponytail, and lint. I got the candy, gum and the rest of the coins. I had the scary job of putting my hands inside the couch; remember we shared our apartment with disgusting bugs and other annoying vermin.

*

In the winter months, most people got "Cabin Fever." The days were short and the bitter winter nights were long and dark. Deep blankets of snow covered the Buckeye tree and first-floor yards. Many times in January our second story porch would get sprinkled with snow. Kathy and I could build snowmen on our porch. When snowplows drove down the streets of the Burg, the drifts of snow covered people's cars. Streetcars had huge sandboxes situated around town so that the sand could be spread along the middle of the street when snow hid the tracks. A few days during the winter schools were canceled. Sometimes people had to stay indoors for days at a time. So whenever there was a break in the weather, people tried to find a cure for "Cabin Fever."

*

Our dad was a resourceful cook. On those days when he couldn't get to work because of a snow day, Dad would grab whatever he could find in the "icebox," and make vegetable soup, spicy spaghetti, pigs in a blanket, or some other hearty meal, depending on what he found hiding on the shelves. Our neighbors could smell the aroma of Dad's suppers by noon and by 6:00 we all took our seats around the dining room table and ate together.

Everyone in our family had a special seat at the table. Dad sat at the head, and Mum sat at the other end. Kathy sat on Dad's right with Kenny next to her. I sat on Dad's left with Pete sitting next to me. Mum had her sons on either side, and Dad had his girls. We always began meals with Grace, "Bless us, oh Lord, for these thy gifts...."

Mum passed the Wonder bread and butter first, and then we could start to eat. My family talked and laughed and shared at our supper table. If I didn't like something, Dad would say, "Take a bite and if you don't like it, I'll finish it for you."

I was a very picky eater. I didn't like fat from steak, skin on chicken, vegetables—or for that matter anything green, liver—fried or in turkey stuffing, nuts—in cookies or alone, or blueberries fresh or in pancakes. Most of the time Dad cleaned my plate after he finished his own. He'd wipe up all the bits of food with a crust of the bread and then see if Kathy needed help with cleaning her plate. Probably, because of my finicky food habits, I was very skinny when I was a kid living in the Burg. On the other hand, Dad was always on the heavy side of the scales.

*

Forty years later when Mum came to live with me in her old age, she'd ask, "I didn't cook much, did I? Kenneth did most of the cooking."

I'd laugh and reassure her, "Mum, we never starved, even when Dad lost his job we never starved...."

*

Kathy and I waited on the porch until we saw the 75 streetcar stop and let Dad off at 5:30. Then he'd wave up at us, and we raced to the front door. As soon as Dad walked inside the apartment he was greeted with hugs and kisses from his three girls. He'd walk down the long hallway and ended up in our front room. Finally, Dad sat in his comfortable green chair. Kathy and I pulled off his shoes and socks so that he could stretch his aching toes.

Besides that old green couch, we had another interesting piece of furniture. My family had acquired an unusual, small screen, black & white television set that sat in the corner of our living room for many years. On those cold dark evenings, Dad lit the gas logs in the fireplace and Mum, and the boys sat on the green sofa to watch the television shows. Dad enjoyed the "Friday Night Fights." After dinner, my sister and I sat on the rug on either side of Dad as he watched the fights. Now the strange thing about our television was that it flipped, and flipped and flipped. Not the television, but the black & white pictures on the screen. We got used to it, and that's how we spent our cold winter evenings, together staring at the flipping television.

*

Since I was born in January, ten days after Christmas, my parents tried to make my birthdays special even though they spent most of Dad's paycheck for Christmas gifts. My dad would take off work to cook a big dinner and invite all the relatives to my birthday parties, which were always celebrated on January 3rd; no matter what day the date fell. My Godmother, Peggy always remembered my birthday when I was a kid. Peggy and Ray were great Godparents. Kathy's Godparents forgot her birthday presents, maybe because they had ten kids and Joe and Ann couldn't remember that Kathy was born on Halloween.

January 3rd was always the date in which school kids returned to school after the first of the year. Occasionally we'd go back to school on the 4th of January but for the most part, it was on my birthday. I don't think anybody should go to school on their birthday.

When I was in the fourth grade, I had my first "friends" get together. On the last day of school before Christmas break, I invited all the girls in my class to my party. That year January 3rd was on a Sunday. So I asked everyone to come on the Saturday before my birthday. I hoped everybody could make it to the party, so I gave each girl an original invitation made especially for her. I knew that Mary Beth couldn't make it to my party because we shared the same birthday. I guess her father wasn't as good a Catholic as mine because her name wasn't Genevieve. Every girl giggled and promised that she'd come to my party, but at 1:00 only three friends showed up at the apartment.

Their mothers stayed and celebrated my birthday too.

I had so much fun at my birthday party. The girls laughed and pointed every time I showed them something interesting about our apartment, so I thought they were having fun too. I showed them my room that I shared with my little sister, Kathy. Over the years, Kathy and I had drawn beautiful pictures of all of our favorite things on the walls surrounding our bed. We played three games, pin the tail on the donkey, musical chairs and run up and down the fire escape. Each girl won a prize that Mum and I had bought at the 5 & 10-cent store the day before my party. I opened my presents. I remember I got a pink jewelry box from my parents, but I don't remember what my friends got me. Right after the chocolate cake and vanilla ice cream were severed, the girls and their mothers hurried home.

The next Monday, I took my jewelry box to school to share, but Sister Mary Emmett told me to take it home before it got broken. So I kept it in my plaid book bag. Mary Beth couldn't share her silver cross necklace either, even though it was more religious than my jewelry box. I usually walked the two blocks home for lunch every day, but I begged Mum to let me buy my lunch at school. Mary Beth and I sat in the school cafeteria together eating our chicken noodle soup and examining the compartments of my new jewelry box. Mary Beth let me wear her necklace until afternoon recess.

We were eating on the benches behind my three friends who had come to the party. Suddenly I heard Bridget say, "Mrs. Schumacher," and something about my party. I guess she didn't know that I was behind her because they didn't stop the gossip. Bridget snickered as she described to the others how old my mother looked. In a loud whisper, she giggled and told her friends that Mum looked like her grandmother. The three girls cackled like a bunch of mean hens.

Marie answered back, "My mother hinted that Mrs. Schumacher must use a red hernia rinse on her hair because she is too old to have naturally colored red hair."

As I was finishing my chocolate milk, Anna recounted to her pals that, "As soon as we walked down those dreadful flights of stairs and got to the sidewalk, Mother threw that "prize" to the curb. Mother said that the fake jade comb and brush set was junk from the 5 & 10¢ store. Our new Buick's whitewall tires crushed them when Mother pulled out into the street." They all had a laugh at that story.

Bridget repeated to her friends what Mrs. McCoy disclosed to her on their way home from my party, "Mommy said, 'Genevieve's family is so very poor, and that's why her family has to live in those dilapidated apartments. Everyone knows that people on the other side of the tracks are unfortunate and need Christian charity.'"

The more the girls chattered about my party, the sadder I got. To make matters worse, after lunch Sister decided to move our seats for the month.

She seated us according to the latest spelling test grades. 100%'s in the first row and in descending order all the way to the last row, back seat for me. At least, if anyone noticed, they might think I was crying because of the 55% spelling test grade. I couldn't wait to run home.

When I got home, I let Mum know that next year, I wanted a family party for my birthday. That's the way we celebrated my birthdays from then on. My dad always cooked my favorite meals until he died when I was sixteen. Every birthday was filled with love and family; the way birthdays should be celebrated.

REMEMBER

Be with the people who love us, and the people that don't like us, don't matter.

FEBRUARY days were cold and too short.
Most of the time we stayed indoors.
The afternoons were perfect times to read
Nancy Drew books or
Listen to Elvis records on my portable record
machine.

After fourth grade, most of my friends lived in "The Annex" or in "The Colonial" apartment building next door. An alleyway separated the two apartment buildings. The tenants whose apartments faced the alley had fire escape like porches. Below the porches in the alley where trash bins, although most of the garbage in the Colonial was incinerated by George, the janitor.

The two apartment buildings shared the alley with about six single dwelling homes. Those people's backyards were at the end of the alley. Mrs. Meyers chain-link fenced her property all the way around. She had a son named Frankie, but he wasn't allowed to play with the Alley Rats. That's what the kids were called who lived and played in the alley.

The rest of the people, who lived in those single homes, never came out that back way, or at least, we never saw them.

The only time cars or trucks entered the alley was when they made U-turns near the garbage cans or when someone moved in or out of the buildings. People would say, "The Midnight Movers came last night." Then we knew that another family had skipped out on a couple of months rent during the dead of night. So for the most part, the alley belonged to the kids.

There were probably 50 families living in the two buildings most of the time when I was a kid. Most people moved in and in a few months left when things got better for them. My parents had lived in the Annex since the 1930s'. I was the only Genevieve that lived in the neighborhood, but we had many Kathys. Kathleen, Catherine or Katherine were very popular names for some reason in the 1950s'. I was named after a very holy saint, but I don't know why there were so many Kathys in the two buildings. Because of this, every Kathy actually had two names when we were hanging around with each other.   My sister was KathySchumacher, spoken as if her name was one word. Our circle of close friends was KathyKelly, CathyannConway, KathieO'Brien, KathySturk, KathieBergman, and CathyNovak.

*

In the wintertime, we usually hung out in the lobby of the Colonial. The Colonial had once been a famous men's hotel. At the main entrance were two sets of double glass doors, so that the cold wind or hot, humid air could not enter the building. When you came in from the front entrance, you saw two large marble pillars holding up the building. The lobby looked like a church to us, but without all the statues, crucifixes and stained glass windows.   The floors were polished imported marble from Italy. The high ceilings had beautiful, faded pictures painted upon it by artists who had died long ago. Halfway down the long, wide, hallway was two wooden niches where we could hide when we played release, which is similar to hide & seek. The lobby was warm and safe, so in the wintertime, most of my friends played there. We'd act out plays, or play dress-up and have breathtaking weddings. From time to time we'd sing songs with the transistor radio. The echoes made our singing sound rich and pure. At the end of the lobby was the winding staircase that went up to the apartments. Many times we played on those stairs. Sometimes we helped older people carry shopping bags loaded with groceries way up to the fourth floor. The building had an elevator, but no one remembered when it was in service, not even George, the janitor. And he had been working at the apartments since my two older brothers had roamed these same hallways.

George was a huge kindhearted black man. He was the only black person I knew or saw until I went to the public high school. All the kids liked George, and he always had a big toothy smile for us kids. George let us play in the lobby, in hallways, and in the basement washrooms of the Colonial. Just like the Kathy's had two names that always went together; "George the janitor" was what we called George. Even after he was promoted to manager, the Alley Rats still called him, "George, the janitor," because that was his name.

When George was promoted to manager, he and his stately wife came to live in one of the rear apartments at the very back of our alley. I remember when they moved in. A big green truck pulled into our alley and slowly made its way to the dead end. All the Alley Rats chased after the truck. When George, the janitor got out of the driver's side, he had a big old cigar in his mouth. He walked around to the passenger's side and opened the door for his statue-like wife. She looked like a bronze queen as she stepped out onto the snow. She had on a full-length fur coat the color of ginger with a fur hat to match! That was the first and the last time we ever laid eyes on her. Looking back on the early 1960s', I now realize that most of the residents in the building didn't want black people living among us, even if their apartment was way in the back of the apartment building.

*

Besides having friends my age, I had an adult friend, named Mary. She lived on the first floor in apartment number 1. Mary and her husband didn't have any children of their own. We called her husband "Daddy Guy." He worked as a conductor on the passenger trains that passed through our town. Mary liked to take me shopping with her to downtown Pittsburgh on the train. "Daddy Guy" would smile and say, "Hi," to us as he collected the tickets from the other passengers. I was so proud to know him.

Mary was my best friend. When I was four, I memorized her phone number even though she lived downstairs. Mary dragged me to evening prayer services during advent and lent. She was the holiest person I knew. If I had a question about God or the saints, she always took the time to sit down (with a glass of milk and something good to eat) and discuss things with me.

When the aroma of Mary's freshly baked orange cookies found it's way to the second floor, I knew it was time for a visit. I jumped down the stairs two at a time and knocked on her door. Her black lab, Shine, barked and then Mary answered the door. I was always the first to taste her cookies.

Mary also had a calico cat named Patches. That cat was the inspiration for my first book in the Name Giver series, LIFE IN THE BASEMENT WITH MOTHER. When Mary's cat had kittens, I came down to the first floor to visit with them every day after school. The kittens were so darling, and I secretly thought that I could keep the yellow striped one that I had named, "Kitty Tom." As soon as they were old enough I brushed the kittens with a special brush that I borrowed from Kathy. One Saturday after we came home from grocery shopping, we discovered that the kittens had disappeared. When we unlocked Mary's front door, I called for the kittens, but none of the kittens ran to greet us, not even Patches.

I searched high and low, but I couldn't find the kittens. I found their empty box in the kitchen just where it had always been, however, Patches and her adorable babies were gone. Stolen? Kidnapped? I was heartbroken. How could someone sneak into Mary's apartment and take every kitty in her house? A month later poor Patches returned to Mary's front yard all beat up and starving. Mary had her cat fixed, and Patches had a long and happy life living in Mary's apartment.

I never knew what happened to Kitty Tom and his littermates until many years later when Mary confessed that George, the janitor took Patches and her kittens to the shelter while we were out shopping. Patches escaped from George, the janitor's truck and found her way home. I hoped that Kitty Tom and his siblings found loving homes and that they lived happily ever after just like Patches. Mary and I kept in touch until she died at the age of 98, she never changed her phone number, and I never had to look up.

*

The Burg was the best place to grow up in the 1960s'. One of the many reasons that my life was so blessed was the wonderful people who lived in the neighborhood. A special group of those individuals where the shopkeepers. The Annex had tenants who lived in all the apartments, but many buildings in the Burg, like the Colonial, had several interesting shops at ground level and apartments above.

*

When boredom set in, Kathy and I decided to collect pop bottles from our neighbors and exchange the bottles for money at the corner pharmacy. Afterward, we always spent our money at the soda fountain at Botzer's Pharmacy. We'd sip our cherry cokes and read comic books that we bought for 3 for 10¢ (if the covers were ripped off).

It was at the soda fountain that we met "The Dentist." We started chatting over our cherry cokes and his chicken salad sandwich. After we ate, he invited us to come over to his office and get a free checkup—anytime. The Dentist worked above the laundry mat next door to Tony's Market. So one day out of the blue, I said to our Kathy, "Let's get our teeth checked out by the dentist."

Like I explained before, we got bored. Kathy and I walked across Rebecca Street and up the side stairs to the second floor. We walked into the dentist's office and asked him if he could check our teeth. And he did! After that, whenever Kathy and I were bored we'd go up to "The Dentist," and he checked our teeth and told us to come back again soon. We never had a cavity, and we never paid. I don't know why we never paid; maybe The Dentist knew that we were poor. We recommended The Dentist to our friends, and soon everyone we knew went to see the dentist when there was nothing else to do.

My sister and I dropped by to visit with him every few months. We never knew his real name; he was just "The Dentist," to the neighborhood kids. Kathy and I didn't get a cavity until we were much older, so he must have been an excellent dentist.

REMEMBER

Friends of all ages are like a garden with a variety of flowers. Look around every day and notice and appreciate the people that visit your unique garden of friends.

MARCH winds blew into the Burg,
And stayed until April.
I could hear the howling of the March wind
When she rose up through the fire escape shaft
And knocked at my window while I slept.

The Burg had a church on almost every city block. You could say we had 100% more churches than bars because the Burg did not have one bar within the city limits. In fact, as of today, the Burg still doesn't have any bars, that I know about. Maybe that's why our town was the best place to grow up.

Of course, being Catholic, my family went to St. James Catholic Church and school. St. James Church is a beautiful place of prayer. There were three main entrances in the front and many more doors off to the sides. We also had a magnificent chapel downstairs for devotions and special Masses. Many pious priests came and went through the doors of St. James in the sixteen years that I attended church. All the priest and nuns that I knew were devoted to God and the work of the Holy Spirit. I loved the Catholic school. My family was not rich like some of the kids in class. All the girls wore navy blue jumpers with a white shirt, so the uniforms somehow made us seem like equals.

When I was in the third grade, playing school became my favorite activity. Kathy and I were best friends, mainly because I could boss her around. When I came home from school, I made Kathy sit down and learn everything I knew. I even taught her how to read better than me. Of course, like most young Catholic girls, I wanted to become a religious nun. Probably because the only teachers I knew as a child were the Sisters of Charity.

All of my early educational years were spent praying for the canonization of Mother Seaton, the founder of the Sisters of Charity. It was a glorious day in heaven and earth when, finally, Elizabeth Ann Seaton became a saint. Her saint's day is January 4, the day after my birthday. Now if that's not a sign from heaven, that I should become a pious Sister of Charity and inspirational teacher. I don't know what is.

My poor sister, Kathy hated school even before she stepped foot inside the halls of St James Catholic school. She was my first and only student so I might have made a few major mistakes, which may have turned her against learning or anything to do with St. James School. Maybe I was too strict with my baby sister because when she entered the first grade, she turned into a redheaded monster. She bit Sister Philip Neri on the wrist, kicked Fr. Murphy in the shin, ran out of her classroom and out the side door and hid in the bushes. And that all happened on Kathy's first day of school! Whenever Kathy escaped, I was summoned to find her. Kathy never bit or kicked me. I knew most of her hiding places—bathrooms (boys or girls), parking lot between the parked cars, or the bushes near the church. I was the only person that my stubborn sister listened to.

Many times throughout that first couple of years after Kathy started first grade; I was sent for to calm her down. I got pulled out of my classroom many times a week, either to lug her out of the bushes after recess or find her somewhere on the school grounds when she hid from her teachers. My job was to hunt her down and drag her out and then present her to the principal. A few times Mum was called to the office to meet with the principal, Sister Mary Something. However, most of the time I'd have to sit patiently beside my unmanageable sister and keep her attention focused on her frustrated teacher. It was a joyful day at St. James School when Kathy settled into third grade and stayed in her seat most of the time.

Kathy changed after her first communion. She liked school more, and she became a good little Catholic girl. We went to confession every Saturday at 3:00 sharp. "Bless me, Father, for I have sinned."

I began my weekly confession with the same prayer each time. At the end, I was forgiven and instructed, "To sin no more."

Confessionals were small rooms with a kneeler, a curtain on one side, and a picture of Jesus on the opposite wall. One Saturday in March I decided to go to the new priest, Father Wickmanoski. Father visited my fourth-grade class and talked about the life of Jesus. He was tall and had a kind face. I thought that Fr. Wickmanoski would forgive me my sins and send me on my way, just like Fr. Murphy had done the last couple of years. When I was through confessing my sins, Father told me to, "Go in peace." Then Father asked me to do him a favor.

I was honored that Father wanted me to do a kindness for him. Right then and there, I decided that God Himself was guiding me towards the sisterhood, and when I grew up, I had to become a nun. I could be a Sister of Charity, just like Sister Ann Theresa, my third-grade teacher. I could devote myself to Jesus just like our holy nuns do. I would be a missionary and help Indian children. I would.... Go to the corner market and buy Fr. Wickmanoski cigarettes!

On that Saturday in March, my life changed forever. I became a trusted servant of the priest and greater than that, a servant of the One, Holy, Universal, and Apostolic Catholic Church.

Every Saturday after that, Father asked me to buy him cigarettes at the corner market. He'd leave the 20 cents in a dish on top of the small altar in the sacristy. The sacristy was the room where the priests stored sacred objects and got dressed before Mass. I'd leave the pack in the dish when I brought the cigarettes back to the church. This ritual continued until Fr. Wickmanoski was transferred a few years later.

Being a trusted member of the church was a great responsibility for me. I never disclosed to my friends that I bought cigarettes for the priest, but I did take that responsibility seriously. I resolved that I had to show up at the confessional every Saturday, even though I might not have sinned at all during the past week so that I could continue buying Father's cigarettes.

*

A short time after that first Saturday, I thought that it would be advantageous to spy on the other churches. There was St. Stephen's Episcopal Church down the block from the Annex on Franklin Avenue, so I decided that we'd start with that church first.

I held a secret meeting with the two Catholic Kathys, although now that I think about it, CathyannConway might not have been a true baptized Catholic at the time. However, she was my sister's best friend and still is to this day. I told the two Kathys that we had to spy on the Episcopal Church. They thought this was an excellent idea because they liked adventure as much as I did. We gathered pencils and notebooks and headed out to explore and see what we could find.

We had never set foot in any other church except for the Catholic churches that my parents took us for weddings and funerals. I remember Mum informed us that every time you entered a new church you say a prayer and make a wish. I guess all my wishes came true because I was a very happy kid growing up in the Burg. The cold wind pushed us towards our destination as we scampered down Franklin Ave. in the direction of St Stephen's Episcopal Church. When we turned up the narrow driveway next to the church, we discovered that a new family was moving in. This driveway leads up to a small cottage where the minister lives. I guess a new minister was moving in because a green moving truck was parked in the driveway and movers were carrying furniture inside the small multicolored brick house.

God was with us! We hurried past the driveway and right up to the gray concrete church steps. There were three arched stone doorways, and we chose the middle front door. The heavy wooden door was unlocked, so the three of us just strolled right inside like we had done this one hundred times before. We looked around the dark entryway. We didn't see any holy water at the entrance, so I wrote this down in my spy notebook.

#1 No holy water at the door. We saw pews down the middle, an altar at the other end, and stained glass windows along the sides of the walls, but that's where the similarities ended. No statues of Mary or any other saints.

#2 No statues of Mary or St. Stephen. We noticed a poor box just like the one we had at St. James. My sister, Kathy and her friend, CathyannConway both wrote this information down in their notebooks. #1 mitchen box.

When we compared notes, I asked my Kathy what "mitchen" was. Kathy explained to me it was the wooden box that people put money in for the mitchens, just like at St. James. Decades later Kathy disclosed to me more about mitchens, but that's her story to tell not mine.

Soon we forgot about taking notes and concentrated on the spying part of our task. We studied hymnbooks hoping to find clues we could use later on. Some of the hymns were the same as ours, and some were different. We descended underneath the pews and slithered around on the flagstone floor. There were long dark purple cushions on the pews, but no kneelers. We searched for the confessional, but they didn't seem to have the tiny room inside this church. I scribbled in my notebook

3 No confessional—in parentheses, I noted (maybe Episcopalians didn't sin, or maybe they don't admit to it). I swiftly added

#4 No kneelers

#5 Different songs.

I closed the notebook and didn't open it again until after lunch. I didn't want to miss anything on our first run through the church.

During my exploration of a dark corner in the church, I came across a secret door behind a heavy tapestry near the side altar. When I opened the mysterious door, we saw a lighted flight of steps leading downstairs to the basement floor. However they didn't have a chapel like St. James, instead, they had underground rooms. We snuck within the rooms on either side of a lengthy hallway, but there wasn't that much to notice. Towards the end of the hall, there was another set of steps leading up.

When we scrambled up the stairway, we found ourselves in a completely different building behind the church. This part of the building was where their top-secret offices were located. We had discovered the heart of St Stephen's Episcopal Church. People were talking. We eavesdropped, but they didn't disclose anything about St. James or Catholics or any other thing that seemed significant to three young spies.

St. Stephen's Episcopal Church had lost some of its excitement by then. For that reason, we decided to run for it and find an exit. We located a door and scrambled out into the windy street on the backside of the church. We were sure we would come back another time and bring more spies. Maybe next time we could widen our search and find something worthy of note.

In the weeks that followed, we learned the secrets of St. Stephen's. We found restrooms, changing rooms for the brides and grooms, storage rooms, and the minister's personal office. We identified every square inch of that church. We made a basement map with detailed information about the area, the location of rooms, and inventoried interesting stuff that we found in each place.

Now it was time to get back home. Mum would have to fix us some Campbell's chicken noodle soup and maybe after lunch, we could visit Mary. She liked to bake cupcakes on Saturday afternoons.

REMEMBER

Explore the world around you. Learn all that you can, when you experience something new. You never know when that information might come in handy later on in life.

MAY days were sunny and bright.
The nights were warm enough to open
The fire escape windows,
So that the breeze might come in.
It rained, but not too much.
Mary's garden started to bloom.
Spring was in the air!

When my older brothers, Pete and Kenny were "only children" (growing up without Kathy and me), they never had a pet. The main reason given was that Mum was allergic to furry animals. However, I think that Pete and Kenny didn't try hard enough to get pets, because when Kathy and I came along; we had our share of dogs and cats and a few non-furry creatures.

I was about seven years old when Dad had to go to Florida; I think he won a cooking contest. His hobby was cooking, so in his spare time, he was the chef in the family. When he came back home, Dad told Kathy and I that he bought us each pet.

"But, Daddy, Mum is allergic to pets," we most assuredly cried out together.

However, Dad stated to us that these pets didn't have fur. Daddy was excited about this animal, but his lips were sealed. He would not tell us what it was until they arrived.

We didn't wait too long because sure enough when I got home from school a few days later, two of the most stunning animals (without fur) were swimming in our crystal punch bowl. The tiny pair was bobbing up and down in the water. Kathy was excited. She notified me that the bigger one was mine, and the smaller one was hers, and we had to name them quickly. "If they don't have names, they won't come when we call them."

Just about then, Mum joined us and enlightened us about some fascinating facts about our new pets. First, the boys carry the babies in their pouches and give birth to about 20 to 30 children. Wow! Soon we might have 32 beautiful creatures swimming in our crystal punch bowl. I could tell the boy was carrying babies because he was fatter around the middle and he was tilting a bit in the water. Mum had put some plants in the water, and our pets curled their long thin tails around the plants.

Mum also told Kathy and me that our seahorses have to eat shrimp. She held up a small clear packet that looked like it had very tiny gray seeds inside. The packet contained the shrimp eggs, so Mum poured a few eggs into the water, but nothing happened. Our pets didn't chase the eggs to the bottom of the punch bowl; they stayed attached to the plants. Then, Mum sprinkled a bit more in the water, still nothing happened. We thought we should wait awhile and see if any of the eggs hatched so that our two seahorses could have some yummy shrimp to eat.

While we waited, Kathy and Mum talked about some good names: Tom & Jerry, Pete & Kenny, Ken & Gen. For me the answer was simple because that very day Fr. Murphy visited my classroom and taught us the Bible story about Sampson's long, strong hair and Delilah's beauty. As a result of that Bible lesson, I decided that our exceptional seahorses should have strong biblical names. Kathy and I made sure that our out-of-the-ordinary pets were baptized with the names Sampson and Delilah.

It seemed that Kathy and I were the first generation in our long family history to have acquired any breed of pet. No one in our family had experience in the care and feeding of furry animals, let alone the supervision of two seahorses from Florida. We left that duty to Mum. She was a registered nurse, although in the 1950s' she stayed home and took care of our family.

Soon the shrimp hatched, and hatched, and hatched. There were so many miniature pink shrimp in the crystal bowl that it was hard to see Sampson and Delilah. Instead of eating the hundreds of shrimp, the hundreds of shrimp were attacking our cherished pets!

We discovered too late that:

#1 Seahorses need an air pump to keep the water oxygenated.

#2 Seahorses only need a few shrimp eggs a week.

We learned too little too late. By then, the last memory I had left of our first pets was their beautiful little bodies floating on top of the still water, eaten by hundreds of hungry baby shrimp. I silently cried as I scooped Sampson and Delilah out of the punch bowl with a tablespoon. A nurse or not, Mum couldn't do the deed. Kathy briefly wanted to keep the tiny shrimp as pets but...how could we keep these brutal creatures? The shrimp went down the kitchen drain, with no sad goodbyes or tears.

*

Dad smoked cigars. He liked the two for a dollar El Producto in a glass tube. He collected the glass tubes because my dad liked to save all kinds of coins. Silver dimes fitted perfectly inside the tubes. As I looked at Samson lying on the spoon, with his 30 children sleeping inside his lifeless pouch, I knew exactly what to do. We must have a Christian burial for Samson and Delilah and their children.

The funeral will be at Pup-Pup and Grandma Ryan's house on the top of Mill Street. Pup-Pup was sick at the time, and Grandma liked us to visit. Kathy and I got the holy water from inside the wooden crucifix that hung above our parents' bed. We also took the candles and oil. This crucifix had everything that we needed for the funeral. It was The Last Rites Crucifix, used to give the Sacrament of the Dead.

I gently placed the body of Delilah on some toilet paper and wrapped her up just like an Egyptian mummy. When it was Samson's turn, I decided to pour a bit of holy oil on the toilet paper and wrap him tighter so that the babies stayed inside his pouch. We placed the bodies inside their individual glass tubes. After that, we covered the cigar tubes with a washcloth. Then we put the wrapped cigar tubes inside a lunch bag and headed uptown to Grandma's house. Mum phoned ahead to let everyone know that there was going to be a seahorse family funeral on Mill Street.

Our cousin, Maryann, was ready for us when we walked up the hill and opened the storm door. She had already dug two deep holes in the backyard near Grandma's rose bushes. She also had found some scraps of cotton cloth from Grandma's sewing chest. Maryann was a year older than me and very smart for her age. She knew many interesting facts about many subjects. One of the details that Maryann knew was, "Egyptians didn't wrap their rulers in toilet paper; they used cotton cloth, Egyptian cotton cloth, to be exact!"

Maryann insisted that she examine the bodies before we mummified them. So I carefully unwrapped the toilet paper as Maryann and Kathy repeated a prayer in Latin, "The Our Father." Kathy then sprinkled the holy water on Samson and Delilah's tiny remains, and I rewrapped our precious gifts from the sea in the Egyptian cotton cloth.

Maryann anointed the mummies with holy oil and slid them into the two tubes. We stuffed the tubes with fresh toilet paper more holy water and topped them off with red & pink petals from Grandma's rosebushes. Then I carefully sealed the glass tubes with the plastic caps. Maryann gently placed the tubes inside the freshly dug graves and just as we were about to cover the holes; I remembered something that we had forgotten to do.

We needed to write a eulogy about Sampson and Delilah and place the note inside each of their personal tubes. Maryann ran and got a pen and paper from her room upstairs.

I wrote the eulogy:

HERE LIES DELILAH.

WIFE AND MOTHER.

A BRAVE AND HOLY SEAHORSE.

XOXOXOXOXOXOXOXOXOXOXO

HERE LIES SAMSON.

HUSBAND OF DELILAH.

FATHER OF HIS MANY CHILDREN.

EATEN BY SHRIMP.

DIED IN THE PRIME OF HIS LIFE.

WE WILL MISS HIM.

Kathy thought that Delilah's eulogy was too short. But too bad, it was late afternoon, and we had to walk home soon. Finally, Kathy and I rolled up the scrolls and tied a white ribbon around each scroll. As we were doing that, Maryann dug up the glass tubes for the last time and opened their coffins. She pulled out the rose petals, toilet paper, and mummies. We placed the seahorses gently inside the scrolls and refilled the tubes with more fresh rose petals and toilet paper. At last, we sealed the glass coffins with the stoppers and buried our dearly loved pets.

I'm sure that they are still at peace, deep in the ground in the backyard of our Grandma Ryan's old brick house on Mill Street in the Burg.

*

My sister and I had many animals come into our lives after the seahorses. Our next pets were Easter peeps. When I was a kid the 5 & 10¢ stores sold tiny yellow chicks for Easter. One Saturday afternoon I found two dimes in the green couch and rushed out the door to the store to find out how many peeps I could get for two dimes. I had just enough to buy two peeps. Even though I knew that they were girls, I named them "Pete and Kenny."

Pete and Kenny followed me around the apartment the moment we came home together. They'd scamper to me when I called them. I loved Pete and Kenny with all of my heart. After about a month, Daddy put cage wire around the porch railings because Pete and Kenny could not be trained to go to the bathroom on the newspaper.

We had the chicks for about three months. They grew tall and fat. The Sturk's lived on the third floor, and their porch overlooked ours. Mr. Sturk complained to George, the janitor, so George notified Mum that the chickens had to go. Walter felt bad because he came over to our apartment to play with the chicks, but his father explained to him that, "poultry had no place in this apartment building!"

A few frantic phone calls were made to the relatives. It was explained to me that Pete and Kenny would be much happier if they lived with the

McMuldren's. So the next Saturday, my brother, Kenny, packed Kathy and I and my peeps into his Buick, and off we went to our cousins, the McMuldren's. There were ten kids in the family, a few boys, and mostly girls. It just so happened that the middle three girls were around the same ages as Kathy and I. They lived in a big wooden house at the end of a dead end street. Their house had an even larger fenced-in backyard.

I knew I would miss my peeps, but they were near enough to visit by car. We stayed a long time so that the peeps could get used to their new gigantic yard and then we drove back home to the Burg. I felt sad, but I knew that the McMuldren's yard was the best place for my adorable chicks.

I was brave. I kept telling Kathy that we could see Pete and Kenny often since our parents spent almost every weekend playing cards with Ann and Joe McMuldren. Sure enough, the next Saturday we drove to the McMuldren's. Kathy and I jumped out of the car and ran into the yard. We called out to Pete & Kenny, but they didn't come to me. I searched everywhere, but I couldn't find my beloved peeps.

Finally, Ricky came up to us and whispered so that just Kathy and I heard, "We ate your chickens last Sunday for dinner."

No, it couldn't be true! They ate my pets! Kathy and I were devastated. We sat on the tire swings and cried our eyes out while our parents started dealing out the cards.

*

A few years later, Maryann's dog, Shadow, had a litter of cute Cocker Spaniel puppies. We got one of the puppies and named him Smokey. We taught him doggie tricks. We took him on long walks around the block. Kathy and I loved Smokey. But soon, Mum's allergies got too bad to ignore. She developed itchy hives and swollen eyes. While Kathy and I were at school, Mum phoned the McMuldrens. Our parents decided that Smokey would be happier living with them.

"They have an enormous fenced-in yard. He'll be happy with all of the kids playing with him. You girls can visit with Smokey every weekend," Mum tried to explain.

I had heard all of this before, almost word for word, so I blurted out, "No, Mum! Not the McMuldrens!"

I was miserable for a long time, I missed Smokey so much, but he was happier living in a big yard instead of our cramped apartment. Smokey lived a very long and happy life. I saw him far into his old age. Every time we visited our cousins, I'd call out to Smokey, and no matter what he was doing, he always ran to greet us.

REMEMBER

God made creatures great and small. We have to love our animals. But we also have to make decisions for their comfort. Pets have to be happy too.

JUNE days are long and hot and humid.
We can hear the birds sing.
We can hear the kids sing,
"No more pencils, no more books,
And no more teachers' dirty looks." School is out!
Time for fun!

In October, two years before I was born, my dad bought some ground out in the country. Dad and Mum were renters all of their lives, but Dad always wanted to own some land that he could call his. Consequently, one day he came home and told Mum that he had bought 6 acres in Murrysville for $1,000.

After that, every weekend in June and all through the hot summers our family drove to the country. Soon that's what we named the 6 acres, "The Country." Woods and hills surrounded The Country. The land that we owned sloped down from the two-lane road towards a stream. The stream was on flat land with thick woods on one side and a country gas station and small grocery store on the other side. The country store sold cold bottles of pop, ice cream cones, sandwiches, and a variety of other stuff to eat. A big brightly painted sign in front of the store read, "Eat here and get gas!" Whenever we saw that sign, we knew we were at The Country.

The stream that flowed through the ground was too wide to cross without sinking into the mud and losing your shoes like I did many times. One day when our Grandma Schumacher slipped on the pebbles, Dad decided that a bridge must be built. The next Saturday the relatives arrived and by Sunday afternoon, a 10-foot long wooden bridge was built.

Soon after that, Dad decided that we needed a shed to store all our picnic stuff, lawn mowers, and equipment during the week. So one Saturday the relatives arrived and by Sunday afternoon we had a long metal shed big enough to store all our supplies and room enough to get out of the rain when it stormed. There is nothing that sounds more exhilarating than a heavy rain pounding on a tin roof!

Next, Dad decided that we needed an outhouse because even though the woods surrounded us, the women needed a private place to go to the bathroom. So the relatives arrived one Saturday and by Sunday afternoon, the wooden outhouse with two brand new toilet seats was put together with shovels, wood, nails and lots of hard work.

The Country became our home away from home. We arrived early Saturday mornings with enough food and drinks to feed an army of cousins. The first thing we did after we had unloaded the trunk of the car was to bring the drinks to the crick. Some people call a "crick" a "creek" but in the Burg, we called a little stream a crick! Kathy and I built a small dam with rocks and tree branches and then gently placed the case of Iron City Beer bottles and cream soda into the cold water.

When we went to the country, we were never alone. Grandparents, uncles, aunts, cousins, and friends, would drop by for the day and most of the night. The grownups usually played pinochle and drank beer all day.

The kids had the most spacious field of grass and wildflowers that you could ever imagine. My dad mowed the tall grass around the shed so the older cousins could play baseball, croquet, or horseshoes. And there were many wild places where a kid could explore and have a great time in nature. My sister and I picked bouquets of flowers or made three-leaf clover necklaces for hours. Every Arbor Day, Dad bought a tree, and we planted it along the stream. Dad loved The Country; it was a little part of the world that he could truly say that he owned.

Dad had a very special talent. He could tread in any field or yard and find a four-leaf clover. He has been particularly good at finding four-leaf clovers at The Country. All the kids ran out in the open field with my dad to see who might be the first to find a four-leaf clover. Dad won that contest every time he went looking for them. He always gave the four-leaf cover to one of us kids. When Dad gave one to me, I cherished it with all of my heart.

Even out in The Country, I was sent to shop at the nearby store. A few times I went to buy cigarettes for the relatives but most of the time I went to buy some kind of treats for the kids. My father was not only a big guy, but he had a bigger heart to go with it. Whenever we kids cleaned up trash or pick up glass bottles, Dad rewarded us with money. Dad would take out a few bills and hand them over to me and say, "You're the boss, take this money and go buy everybody ice cream cones at the store."

Dad was always making someone the "boss" whenever he wanted something done. We always had a boss for the jobs around The Country or for that matter, at home too.

There was always something to do at The Country. We just never knew what to do first. The

McMuldren girls liked to go down to the crick and dam up the water to make a huge shallow pool so we could cool off. We could splash and sit on the pebbles underneath the cool water and kick our feet until we were exhausted. Or we might create mud pies with flower petal frosting that baked in the hot summer sun. Next, we'd cover each other with mud and be given the best mud baths in the world. We would lie on the banks of the crick, and the warm brown mud would bake and crack on our skin. Then we would jump into the pool of water and start all over again and again.

My sister liked to go hunting in the crick. There were hundreds of minnows and tadpoles, but I loved to hunt crawdads. The best spot to go crawdad hunting was near the wooden bridge. We got two paper cups to trap the small water creatures. We liked to see who could catch the largest crawdads. I was terrified to catch them with my bare hands because of their gigantic pinchers and long antenna. Crawdads hid in the mud and blended in with the dark pebbles on the bottom of the stream, so I had to be careful not to get pinched when hunting for them. Many times we took them home in a glass jar only to have them die in a few days.

Other times my cousins and I raced to the hill at the far end of the property. There on the hillside grew the sweetest strawberries in the world. We'd spread out at the top of the slope and slowly snack our way down to the bottom eating our fill of small wild strawberries. We'd have a bowl in one hand to collect some for the adults, but most of the strawberries belonged to us kids. When I needed a rest from picking the berries, I might plop down on the hillside and look up at the clouds. I'd say, "Look! I see a clown in that cloud," or "Do you see the angle-shaped cloud over there?"

During cloudy afternoons, I could see beams of light shining through the clouds making the rays of light look like fingers as they touched the Earth. The sky reminded me that God was looking down from above and blessing all of us. We never worried about bees, snakes, poison ivy or other dangers that may be in the world today. The Country was heaven for us, and no harm could ever come to us, most of the time.

I never wore shoes at The Country and still don't like to wear them today. One day as I was chasing Kathy across the newly built wooden bridge, I fell on all fours and got about twenty splinters in my hands and feet. Kathy and I pulled most of the splinters out, but a few broke under my skin. I soon forgot all about the remaining splinters embedded in my palms. After a few days, a red streak started sneaking up my arm. I showed the red streak to my cousin, Maryann, because she was wise, and I believed everything that she told me. Maryann informed me that if that red line gets to my heart, I would die, so I ran and showed Mum my infected hands. Maryann was right. I had blood poisoning. Lucky for me, Mum was a nurse and knew what to do.

The worse thing that ever happened to me was when I fell on a broken milk bottle. One day everyone was in the shed waiting for the downpour to stop. As the thunder clapped and the jagged lightning ran across the sky, I wondered if our shed with its tin roof was protected against the lightning. I ran out the entrance to see if we had a lightning rod on the roof. There were two wooden steps just outside the doorway. They were slick with rain. As soon as I stepped on the first step with my bare feet, I fell sideways. I landed on the jagged edge of a broken milk bottle that someone had thrown to the side of the shed. The sharp broken glass cut through the skin of my thigh—boy did I bleed!

My Aunt Lena thought that I needed stitches, but I pleaded with my dad. I was so afraid of needles. So Mum got out the first aid kit and cleaned out the cut with peroxide. She wrapped my leg with a clean cloth and tape. I sat down on the cot inside the shed and soon fell asleep, exhausted from all the bloody commotion. On Monday, I went to the doctor's office. He checked out my wound, but I didn't get stitches because it was too late by then. I still have a four-inch gash in my right leg to remind me of the fun times we had at The Country.

*

At the end of each summer, our family had the "Campbell Clan Reunion." Grandma Ryan was a Campbell before she married Pup-Pup. Grandma had eight brothers and sisters, so any Campbell that was still alive was invited to show up at the reunion if they could. Relatives from all over, including the great state of Michigan, gathered to have an end of the year party at The Country. Some of the young cousins stayed overnight in the shed. Some of the older people came home with us to the apartment. Some might stay with other cousins. The relatives made banners and sang, *"The Campbells are coming, hurray, hurrah! The Campbells are coming, hurray, hurrah!"*

The Campbells loved to sing and drink and have fun. We played games, like tug of war and of course, cards. We roasted hot dogs around the campfire. We got to know second cousins once removed. We laughed and sang until it was time to leave, and then we knew that the summer was almost over. One year my brother, Pete, brought some of his friends to the reunion. When Red O'Leary saw my cousin Liz, it was love at first sight. They got married on my eighth birthday five months later. A few years ago they celebrated their fiftieth wedding anniversary. Red and Liz are still in love!

*

1967 was a sad year for my family for many reasons. We didn't go to the Country anymore because Dad didn't own a car. My dad borrowed Pete's car on the Arbor Day before he died so that we could plant a Cypress tree along the bank of the stream. That visit was the last time we went to The Country as a family. As we pulled off the road, we saw a group of teenage boys playing baseball in our field. Dad got out of the car with the tree in his arms and Mum, Kathy and I followed him with the shovel and our picnic lunch. As I got closer, I could tell that most of the boys were about my age. Dad stopped at home plate and asked the catcher, "Who mowed the grass and made the chalk lines?"

A tall skinny kid with glasses answered and disclosed that his father fixed it for them so that they could play softball. Dad removed his cigar from his mouth and proclaimed, "Well, then you're 'The Boss' because I'm Mr. Schumacher, and I own this place!"

The next summer before I went to college, I got a work-study job teaching Y-camp kids how to swim. I don't know how to swim to this day, but I was a great swim coach when I was seventeen. I met a friendly kid named Tom on the first day at the Y-camp's orientation. As we were talking in the counselor's tent, he divulged something fascinating.

"I live in Murrysville near the 'Eat here and get gas sign.' Get it? Eat here and get gas. Funny," he smiled.

"My family owns 6 acres in Murrysville," I went on.

"Is your last name Schumacher?" Tom asked seriously.

"Yes! How did you know that?" I asked.

"I remember you. I'm 'The Boss'! Your dad

came out to plant a tree when some friends and I were playing ball. He made me 'The Boss,' your dad is cool. How is he?"

"He's Ok," I lied.

Dad had passed away last fall, but I couldn't talk about it to Tom or anyone else for that matter, it hurt too much. It was too soon, and I was too sad.

REMEMBER

"The good old days are now!" You just don't know it yet. Enjoy yourself, eat, sing, dance, play and give thanks for what you have. Get out in nature and smell the flowers.

JULY days were always hot and humid.
The temperature could get up to 95 degrees and
stay that way for days and nights at a time.
The summer rains came at least twice a week.
In the afternoons, we could hear the thunder
And glimpse the lightning shows
That nature put on for us to enjoy.

In those lazy days of summer in the 50s', nobody but rich people had swimming pools. Since we didn't know any rich people, there was a limited way to cool off during those hot July days. We could do three things:

One: fill up the bathtub and have a soak, at least, ten times a day.

Two: walk uptown to the junior high and swim in the indoor pool every weekday from 11:00 until 1:00.

Or Three: walk ten blocks to Frick Park and jump into the fountain.

We tried all three, but during those long hot summer days, a gang of my friends would pack our chipped ham sandwiches and hike to the park. Frick

Park was a kid's dream. We could go to the playground and swing to our heart's content, or make key chains and belts at the crafts pavilion. Surrounding the playground and ball fields was the wonderful woods. There were several trails and paths and The Alley Rats knew them all.

When we arrived at the park, we just had to decide what to do first. Woods or playground? Woods usually won out because it was always cool and shaded under the old, colossal trees. When it rained, the canopy of live branches protected us. Most of the numerous paths twisted down into the heart of the woods. The picnic grounds were at the end of that trail. We called that place, "The Hollow." At the hollow, we had our choice of which trail to pick up from there. Small streams and hills were far and wide, so we explored every part.

The best place to explore in Frick Park was the enormous water fountain on the other side of the park. Because we were city kids, none of us learned how to swim, so the fountain was just right for us. The fountain was about two feet deep and circular in shape, it became our wading pool. Water sprouted up from the middle inviting us to jump in. We didn't have swimming suits, so we just dashed into the fountain in our bare feet, clothes and all, to cool off. When we were tired of running in circles, we could lie on the grassy hill to dry off and eat our lunches. We'd head for home when we got hungry again. Mum never worried about us, maybe because we went in a large group of five or six kids. Life was good at Frick Park.

*

Mr. X was another interesting person who entered our lives when I was a kid in the Burg. Mr. X was the conductor of the 75 Streetcar. He not only collected the money but also steered the streetcar in a big loop around downtown Pittsburgh. Our small town was the beginning and the end of the line. The 75 ran down our street all the way to downtown Pittsburgh. Kathy and I met Mr. X one lazy summer afternoon as we were reading our comic books and drinking our cherry cokes at

Botzer's soda fountain. We noticed a man in a blue uniform patiently waiting for a seat at the busy soda fountain. He had slicked back black hair and shiny sunglasses. He looked like Elvis only older and a bit fatter. I offered him my seat because I knew he was on a tight schedule and I was just wasting time. He smiled and said, "Thank you. Thank you, very much!" Or something like that and took my seat.

My sister, Kathy and I left Botzer's to find a place to read our comic books. We walked towards the front of the Colonial building and sat down on the steps and leaned up against the two pillars on either side of the entrance. My friends Barbie and KathieBergman were singing with the radio in the lobby. Soon we were all reading the comic books. The conductor broke the silence when he came along and surprised all of us by asking if we wanted to take a free ride on his streetcar. We looked at each other and shrugged our shoulders. "Sure," we all said together.

From that day on, we kept our eyes searching for Mr. X, as we called him. Each time Mr. X came to the Burg, the Alley Rats got free rides on the 75 Streetcar to the next town. Then we would hop off and walk home. If it was raining, he'd give us a transfer, and we could walk across the street, and catch the trolley going back towards the Burg. I went downtown shopping many times with Mum or Mary, but the free rides with Mr. X were the ones I remember the most.

*

Most of the time in those humid summers we just stayed close to home. When the roller skate fad happened, everyone needed a pair of adjustable skates. Kathy and I never owned a bike like CathyannConway, but we did have our own roller skates. It seemed like those skates were glued to our saddle shoes. The skates came with a large metal key. Our Mum made us two necklaces out of ribbon to hold the keys securely around our necks. We used the silver keys to tighten the clasps around our toes. A leather strap was wrapped around our ankles to keep the skates on our shoes.

Once we tightened those skates on our black and white leather shoes, we didn't stop unless our foot came out of the metal skate. We raced like the wind around the block. Around and around we'd skate, just like the roller derby ladies on the television.

*

As the days got longer, my friends and I could always find something of interest to occupy our time. For the most part, the alley was the place to be. It belonged to us Alley Rats. On those steaming hot days and long into the evenings, we roller-skated around and around the block. Or we might play jump rope in the alley for hours on end. Other times we played hopscotch, or we dug gigantic holes with our spoons in the backyards of mysterious people we never saw. Other times we would just hang out on their back steps leading up to the neighbors' yards and talk or tell scary stories. The people didn't mind, at least, we didn't think that they cared.

*

Hovering above us on the porch perched like vultures in their armchairs and loungers sat the gossips. These women kept an eye on all of the kids and chitchatted about all the other ladies who didn't sit with them all day. I called them the "first floor gossips." Many times in the summer my friends and I sat quietly on the stairs leading up to the first-floor porch. We would eavesdrop and hear first hand about the malicious rumors that the gossips invented. We learned a lot about the miserable lives of some of the residents who lived in the apartments from those big-mouthed tattletales.

The gossips talked about anyone who wasn't within earshot. They talked about KathieBergman's mother when she was at work. They snickered when they chattered about Mrs. Bergman having to be a housemaid for others and then coming home and making her daughter, Kathie, her slave. KathieBergman did all the housework and grocery shopping at the A&P for the family. On Mrs.

Bergman's days off, the gossips whispered about Mr. Edwards being too fat to come out of his apartment. Even though Mrs. Bergman got paid to do Mr. Edwards shopping and cleaning, she joined in the mean discussion, "If there's ever a fire, he'd have to jump out of his third-story window," they all laughed as they took continuous drags off their filtered cigarettes.

The gossips never ran out of spiteful things to say about people. They pointed at the six blond haired O'Brien kids digging in the yard and uttered that each one of the kids had a different father. They stated that, "Mrs. O'Brien wasn't a Mrs. or even a widow." After Daddy Guy had died at work one afternoon from a heart attack, the gossips spread the insensitive lie that my dear friend, Mary had poisoned her husband's bologna sandwich. My friends and I listened until the gossips talked about someone we cared about, and then we took off to find something else to occupy our time.

I never heard the gossips discuss anything about my parents. Our Mum never visited with those women on the first floor, so I don't think they even knew what Mum looked like. In my long life that I knew my mother, she never ever spoke one unkind or cruel word about anyone. Mum always had decent things to say about everyone she knew. I'd like to think that Mum was only associated with sweet, kindhearted people like herself. Mum used to say, "If you can't say anything nice about a person—keep your mouth shut!"

*

As I said at the beginning of my story, there was a row of small businesses at ground level in the Colonial apartment building next door to our apartment building. All the shops faced the street so that customers stepping off the 75 streetcars or walking past could walk right in an establishment of their choice. Kathy and I played hopscotch on the sidewalk right in front of the shoemaker's shop. We thought that "Joe, the Shoemaker" lived in the back of his shop. We never saw him repairing shoes unless someone was waiting. He was always in the back rooms, except when he stepped outside and walked around to get some fresh air.

Several times a year I found myself inside "Joe, the Shoemaker's" shop. He glued the heels or soles on my father's dress shoes. A sign read, "Work while you wait" on the wall above a shoe rack. He charged 25¢ a shoe and "another quarter if you wanna shine on those shoes...." Whenever "Joe, the Shoemaker" saw Kathy or me playing outside his shoe repair shop, he came outside to say, "Hi."

Now, Joe didn't just say, "Hi, Schumacher girls," and wave. He'd stroll up to us, bend down, and pinch our upturned cheeks, and then he sang, "Shoe, shoe, shooo, mocker."

That's how he greeted us, every time we were near until he closed up his shop in 1967.

When I got married and had kids and grandchildren of my own, I would grab their cheeks and say that same thing. I guess I could see the "Schumacher" in my kids so I would say, "Shoe, shoe, shooo mocker," as I ever so gently pinched their cheeks.

REMEMBER

People spend their time in different ways. Go outside and have adventures. Don't waste time on meaningless tasks. Enjoy the goodness of the people around you. Always try to have fun, but never hurt anyone by what you do or say.

AUGUST days were lazy and hot.
The rain came almost every other afternoon.
We never worried about the weather because we
knew it would be hot and muggy every long day in
August.

One warm August afternoon Barbie, Evelyn, KathieBergman, and my sister and I decided to break the dullness of the afternoon and look for some adventure. When we got bored, there was always the pavilion. The five of us crossed Hay Street and went through the Franklin tunnel. The tunnel and the railroad tracks above it were the dividing lines in the Burg. "Uptown" began at the other end of the tunnel.

On that day, I wanted to bury some shiny new 1962 pennies near the gazebo, so that years later some other adventurer could find the pennies and become rich. The pavilion was a small building with open sides; a small wildflower garden and some young Buckeye trees surrounded the open building.

Anyplace that you sat inside the small building gave you a pleasant view of the outskirts of uptown. The rumble of a train filled our ears as we entered the Franklin Tunnel. I knew just the place to bury the coins, in the dirt that led up to the railroad tracks, near the deep roots of an old Locust tree.

When we had thunderstorms, I liked to sit on the brightly painted benches that circled the low walls inside the pavilion and listen to the calming sounds of the downpour. Most people would run and take cover in the tunnel, but I liked to listen to the rhythm of the rain pounding on the gray roof of the pavilion.

As we strolled through the tunnel towards the pavilion, we heard the laughter of some kids. Three boys from St. James were sitting on one of the colorful benches along the path that led to the pavilion. We girls decided to sit inside the pavilion because even at a young age I knew that redheads shouldn't be out in the sun, not because of sun damage or wrinkles, but because some kids were beginning to call me "Rusty." As in "with all of those freckles, your face looks rusty."

The moment we stepped inside, I noticed a woman sleeping on one of the wooden benches. She rested on her back with a big worn-out purple hat covering her face. The rest of her body was covered with old newspapers. She kind of looked like a Mummy, in a comical way. I had first noticed her last Saturday when I went to confession; she was collecting pamphlets in the vestibule of our church. I also noticed that she did not put any donation into the poor box. At the time, I thought she should be taking money out of the poor box, cause she looked like a vagrant.

When I saw her in our church, I thought that the woman looked like she lived on the streets. Her floppy purple hat covered most of her thick gray hair. She had light blue eyes that darted back and forth. She looked as though she was searching for me as I hid behind the wooden door at the entrance to St. James Church. Her dark purple dress was long but not long enough to hide her painted calves.

She had strange streaks of pink running unevenly up and down her short, stout legs. At her feet, were two paper shopping bags. It was into one bag that she dropped the church pamphlets; I couldn't help but notice that it was crammed with dirty papers of all kinds. "Maybe she picks up rubbish in her leisure time," I thought.

Later I found out that the second shopping bag held all of her earthly possessions, including several bottles of iodine and holy water.

That day when I saw her resting on the bench, my friends and I turned away and tiptoed out onto the garden path. The schoolboys were heading our way, so I sat down on the first bench I saw and fixed my hair into a ponytail. Of course, the boys stopped, and we started to talk about the poor lady on the bench. They had noticed the down-and-out lady napping on the bench earlier. They snickered at her and stated that she was weird snoozing with last week's newspapers covering her like flimsy blankets.

A flash went off in my head; I saw an image of

her inside St. James pocketing the pamphlets about the lives of the saints. I let the boys know that she was a holy woman, a woman that spends a lot more time in church than any of them. "So don't make jokes about her!" I demanded.

Even though I knew in my heart, she may not be all that religious. As far as I knew, she never put a nickel into that poor box to pay for all the pamphlets that she snuck into her shopping bag. She was still an elderly woman, and youngsters shouldn't make fun of the unfortunate. During our chat, the homeless woman woke up and started folding the wrinkled newspapers and placing them into one of her shopping bags. I glanced at her as we flirted with the boys. She gazed in our direction and then occupied herself with her castoffs in the two shopping bags. When she was done arranging things in her bags, she called out to us.

"Hey, you two redheaded girls, are you the Schumacher girls?" Asked the woman in the gazebo.

I was shocked! How could that poor street person know that we were the "Schumacher girls?" Kathy and I were puzzled.   Nevertheless, we ambled over to the bag lady on the bench. Our friends followed us, maybe for protection, but mostly with curiosity.   We surrounded the purple woman and her next words almost made me faint.

Then the dirty, crazy looking bum announced to all of us, "Hi, I'm your Aunt May, on your father's side. Go tell Genevieve there will be one more for dinner tonight. What time does Kenneth get home from the furniture store?"

"The streetcar comes around five-thirty," whispered Kathy.

I couldn't believe it, but on the other hand, we did have many "aunts and uncles." However, I never met her at any of our reunions at the country. And, I could never forget her!

Kathy and I raced all the way home and up the stairs.   Our brother, Kenny was entertaining Mum with one of his wild stories, as she ironed his starched dress shirts. "You'll never guess whom we just met," I declared, more to my brother than to my mother.

If Kathy and I didn't know about "Aunt May," I was pretty sure Kenny didn't either, even if he was fifteen years older. I knew he couldn't have heard about "Aunt May," because at some point during my eleven years of living, Kenny would have made quite a story about Dad's older sister living in the streets, with pink painted legs and black dirt packed in the corners of each blue eye.

We tried to explain as best we could to Mum and Kenny what the bag lady did and said. Was she truly our long lost Aunt May? Yes, and no was the answer. She was our dad's second cousin once removed and then some. Our Mum and Dad knew May quite well, it seemed. Well, Mum knew Aunt May good enough for Mum to tell Kenny to go to the pavilion and fetch her to our apartment.

"Aunt May" made herself at home on our green treasure chest of a sofa after she sprinkled holy water all over our home. She used up a whole bottle as she walked down the hallway and into the living room. May's first visit reminded me of a procession in church during lent—purple vestments, holy water, and strange smells…. There won't be any spare change in between the sofa cushions when she left. That was for sure!

Dad got off the streetcar around six o'clock, and he seemed really happy to see May. After dinner, Dad told May he could call her daughter, Peggy, and tell her May was with us. However, May declared that she had a place to sleep and not to bother about Peggy. May explained to us that even though Peggy was her only child, she was a spy for the government.

Then "Aunt May" explained why her legs were painted pink and why her two shopping bags were full of paper and church pamphlets. In May's mixed-up mind, most people worked for the government and wanted to catch her so that they could get valuable information from her. But May knew how to trick the spies. The iodine prevented X-rays from detecting her. The ink in the newspapers and pamphlets kept her safe from demons when she slept. I found out that May thought if she stayed inside a Catholic church she was protected from the devil and spies. "Aunt May" was more entertaining than our blinking TV. Even Kenny was speechless as May recounted her unbelievable tales.

After May had left our apartment and I guess, headed back toward the gazebo, Dad told us that May was his cousin. When she was younger, she was very smart and worked for the government as a secretary. A few years ago her boss got fired and went to prison for selling secrets to the Russians. The stress was so bad for May that she "cracked up" and hasn't been the same since. After Dad had shared his story, we all felt sorry for May. Except, soon our feelings changed.

A few days later on a hot, humid morning on our way to the Jr. High swimming pool, we saw May sleeping on the bench in the pavilion. In the afternoon when we got home, May was sitting on our sofa telling Mum that there were demons in our home.

"The demons are especially intense around young Kenneth," she constantly warned our poor mother.

From that day on "Aunt May" stayed at our apartment from the moment she woke up until it was time for Kathy and me to go to bed. May either slept at the pavilion or rode the streetcar number 75 to places unknown. On May's daily visits, she spent her time following Mum around the house; telling Mum that her son was evil, and her two innocent girls were spies. I guess May spotted me behind the church doors on that Saturday when I first laid eyes on her. Although I wasn't spying, I was making sure she didn't steal the money from the poor box. My Dad couldn't find it in his heart to tell May to stop dropping by the apartment for hours at a time. "She has to eat," Dad said. "And she is my cousin."

Mum was too easy going to yell at May and tell her to stop with the crazy talk. Mum was a nurse and had worked on a psych ward before she married Dad. So even Mum understood that May was not right in the head.

Every time Kenny brought his shirts home to be ironed, Aunt May drove him nuts with her chatting about his sins. After about a month of May telling Kenny that he was wicked, Kenny had it! My brother got tired of holy water being sprinkled on him every time he sat at the dining room table. Kenny couldn't visit with his own mother without May shouting prayers at him, trying to rid the house of demons. Kenny decided to do something drastic about the May situation. He decided "Aunt May" had to go!

So one day when he brought over his dirty shirts for Mum to wash and iron, he alerted us to his crazy plan. Kathy and I were to keep our eyes open for May from the porch. Occasionally May rode the 75 Streetcar that passed by our apartment building like clockwork every hour. We didn't have long to wait, because there she was, getting off the Streetcar and heading in our direction loaded down with fresh holy water and several bottles of iodine. Kathy and I ran inside to the dining room and informed our persecuted brother that May was on her way for another uninvited visit. By now, May would just let herself into the apartment without knocking on the unlocked door. We heard her yell out to our Mum, "Genevieve, Oh Genevieve."

My brother was ready for his greatest performance. Kenny, the greatest actor in the history of his mind, was in his glory. He had a duty to the family to rid us of our fanatical Aunt May, or else! We were all in our places. Mum was ironing sheets in the dining room. Kenny was sitting in a chair just biding his time until the verbal attacks started. Kathy and I were at our places eating Neapolitan ice cream at the dining room table waiting for Kenny to perform at his best.

After May poured the bottle of holy water over Kenny's head, and he didn't move a muscle, she walked over to Mum and announced for the one-hundredth time, "That boy has the devil in him. What are you going to do, Genevieve?"

Mum was tired of May's visits too, but Kenny surprised all of us by what he did next. He jumped up from his chair and started yelling as he messed up his hair shouting, "I'm the devil, I'm bad, really bad!"

Kenny ran up to Aunt May and whispered something horrible in her ear. Then he ran over to me and picked me up by my short curly hair and pulled me straight out of my chair. Both of our brothers could pull Kathy and me up by our hair. The trick was for me to hold on to Kenny's arms as he pulled up. It was our family trick. With the spoon in my mouth and the bowl tipped over on the table, I wailed, "Let me finish my ice cream. I'm not done with my ice cream!"

Our Kenny was on a mission. He swung me by the hair as he ran around in a circle through the dining room, kitchen, and living room. Around and around he went, holding me by the hair. Kathy got the kitchen broom and chased after Kenny saying, "Let her go! Let her go! Her ice cream will melt."

Mum then pulled the iron's plug out from the wall switch and started chasing Kenny, Kathy and me. Mum was yelling, "Kenny put her down, stop it. Stop it, Kenny," Mum had the hot iron in one hand, and she was trying to grab Kenny's shirt with the other hand. Every time we passed her, Aunt May threw holy water on Kenny. He would yell, "It burns, the devil's in me. I like it! I like it!"

Then Kenny jumped up on the dining room table and dropped me. I crawled over to my ice cream dish and just like a cat eating from a bowl; I licked the melted ice cream. Kathy was swatting Kenny with the broom. Mum was waving the iron at him while I finished lapping up the rest of the melted ice cream. That's a picture I'll never forget. However, the best part was May's expression and what she yelled out next, "This family is mad. You people are all crazy. I'm leaving, and I'm never coming back!"

Aunt May never did come back. That night Dad called Peggy and told her that May was in the Burg. Soon after that Kathy and I waited on the front stoop of our building for Peggy to drive down Hay Street. She arrived in a big, black Cadillac car. Peggy was the exact opposite of her mother, May. Kathy thought that Peggy was a movie star when she got out of her car. Peggy was dressed in red high heel shoes and wore a beautiful red silk dress. When Peggy waved at us, we noticed a huge diamond ring on a red polished finger. Peggy followed my sister and me upstairs to our apartment. After a while, Dad and Peggy left to find May. They found May at the pavilion. Peggy took May home to live with her in a huge home with Peggy's rich husband. That night May was out of our lives, just as fast as she entered it.

A few days later, Peggy phoned to ask if May had shown up around the apartments. May took off again and as far as I know, she was never heard from again.

REMEMBER

Be good and kind to everyone. You never know, that homeless person may be related to you. Treat others, as you would like to be treated. Unless they are mean to you.... then get that person out of your life!

SEADECEMBER days were still warm and humid,
But the days were getting shorter and the nights
turned cool.
Summer was over —
The year was winding down.

When I became a teenager in 1964, I didn't play around in the alley anymore. My friends and I would hang out on the front stoop of the Annex. We'd listen and sing with the rock' n' roll music on my transistor radio. When a noisy train past by, we stopped our singing to count the coaches with the passengers inside, wave to the caboose, and then shout out the number of boxcars that we had counted.

One of those lazy September days will always be etched in my memory. KathieBergman, Barbie and I were sitting on the stoop feeding the pigeons pieces of sugar cookies. The birds swooped down from the roof above us and caught the bits in their beaks as we threw the food at them. Then the birds would fly up to the edge of the roof and eat in peace.

We were laughing at two pigeons fighting over an extra large piece of cookie when I turned my head and glimpsed Billy and his older brother Bobby walking toward us. Their mother, older sister, and two younger brothers had moved into the Colonial during the summer. Billy liked to walk into the tunnel at night and sing sad songs. He didn't like it much at home. Billy had a beautiful voice and a cute face. I had a crush on him, but I didn't think that he knew it.

The brothers walked right up to us and started talking about the music that we were listening to on my transistor. Billy asked me if I liked the new Gene Pitney song, *It Hurts to be in Love*. I let him know that, "Gene Pitney was the best, even if Barbie and KathieBergman loved the Beatles. Gene Pitney was a much better singer and writer. And Gene was an American, not a Brit."

Billy totally agreed with me. I knew immediately that we could be friends. We had, at least, one good thing in common—great music! That afternoon was unforgettable for me. We were talking and laughing and throwing crumbs to the pigeons. Then Billy quietly said that he wanted to tell me something that Barbie had revealed to him. I stood up and looked into his adorable green eyes. Billy pulled me over beside the brick wall of our building, and I thought he was going to whisper in my ear because he bent his head near my check. When all of a sudden, a dirty pigeon squatting above us on the edge of the roof, felt the urge to go to the bathroom. Since pigeons just go when and where they like, that bird decided to let it go right above our heads!

"Splat! Smack! Plop!"

One minute I was talking to a dreamboat boy named Billy and the next minute I was covered with gooey gray pigeon poop—running down my hair, dripping on my face, and soaking through my blouse. I turned away from Billy and ran upstairs so fast I was a blur. I locked myself in the bathroom and didn't come out for 2 hours. I used four bathtubs of hot water and a few bars of Ivory soap too. (We didn't have showers in those days.)

I stayed in the apartment for a week. I was so humiliated. After the disaster, Billy came up to the apartment several times, but Mum let him know that I didn't want to go outside. Billy visited every day, but I couldn't look him in those compassionate green eyes. On the fifth day, I hesitantly spoke to him behind the locked door. When I did come out, we sat on the upstairs hallway steps close to the apartment, just in case anyone else climbed the stairs. Billy never mentioned the pigeon episode because he knew that incident wasn't amusing to me—yet. We became friends, and later Billy became my first love. We are still friends to this very day.

*

That year was a sad time for my family and especially our father. Dad's brother, Uncle Edmond passed away in the late summer. He stepped on a rusty nail and soon died of a rapid infection. Maybe Dad cried before, but I never saw or hear Dad ever shed a tear until the day his older brother passed away. One month after my Uncle Edmond's death, his son, Philip, died of walking pneumonia. We were gone from the alley for about five days after Philip died.

When my family returned home, I learned that poor Mrs. Poland had a breakdown. That week our generous neighbor pitched her pickle jars with all of her coins out her bedroom window. All the Alley Rats went wild picking up the coins that rained down into the alley. Too bad we missed that one, I thought.

Mrs. Poland was taken away to a mental hospital, and she never came back. Mr. Poland wasn't the same after his wife left.

*

In the autumn of my thirteenth year, the gossips started rumors about me. Of course, I wasn't snooping on them at the time, but I heard about the scandalous accusations anyway. The gossips lied about me smoking cigarettes in the basement. They whispered that I was smoking with the two brothers, Bobby and Billy. They said that I was boy crazy and that I was a bad influence on their children. As a result of these malicious lies, none of their daughters were allowed to hang out with me. The rumor wouldn't have been too terrible if my cherished friend, KathieBergman wasn't one of those teenage girls.

KathieBergman didn't come right out and tell me about her mother's decision. I got many hints on the day I came home from the funeral. I knocked on her apartment door to see if she could come outside. I wanted to tell her about the gloomy wake for my 19-year-old cousin. Kathie didn't open her door; instead, she informed me that she had to clean. Like hundreds of times before, I told her that I could help "red up" her house. That means clean the house.

"I'll help you," I replied "I want to tell you about the sad memorial Mass for my cousin. Last week was too depressing. Philip was only 19 years old. All of us couldn't stop crying our eyes out...."

"No, after I red up, I have to go grocery shopping," Kathie whispered from behind the locked door.

"Do you want me to hang around and we can walk to the A & P together?" I asked.

However, she then stated, "I have to do my homework. And I don't need any help. So just go. Ok?"

I didn't know what had happened, so I went down the stairs to the lobby floor to Barbie's apartment. Barbie was the one who informed me that they couldn't hang out with me because I was a bad influence. She let me know that the gossips spread the word that they saw me smoking in the basement with some boys a few days ago.

"But that couldn't have been me! I just came back from my cousin's wake. I wasn't even in town last week!" I cried wiping the tears away from my face.

Barbie shrugged and blurted out, "I'm sorry, but all the mothers ordered their kids not to hang around with you anymore."

I went home and cried on my bedspread until it was soaked. I lost all of my childhood friends, and I didn't do anything wrong. I wasn't even in town! I never would smoke and never have, although I did like Billy. I washed my face and told my Kathy what had happened. Kathy was shocked and said that I could hang out with her, but instead I went downstairs to hunt for Billy. I still had school friends. Besides, soon after that, I had Billy as my first boyfriend.

Evelyn moved away soon after school started and a new girl moved into Evelyn's old apartment. Audrey didn't mind that I was boy crazy because she was too! Even though I was forbidden to hang out with Barbie and KathieBergman, I found out that I still had friends. The other Kathys were my friends. Besides, most mothers didn't believe a word that the gossips spoke, especially KathyO'Brien's mom. Mum never found out, and that was all right with me.

*

Most of my new friends were older but just as enjoyable. We'd hang out on the stoop and listen to music and talk, just like I used to do. One afternoon as my sister and I were counting the boxcars on a very long train, we saw a strange sight. A very short, and very plump woman was exiting the Franklin tunnel. She carried two heavy-looking shopping bags in each chubby hand. The woman would start to amble a bit and then stop every few steps to catch her breath and wipe her forehead with a large hankie. I never saw this woman before so I knew that she didn't live in either of the buildings or in our neighborhood.

I could tell right away that the fascinating lady needed help with her groceries, so I stood up and dragged my sister, Kathy with me. We walked up to the woman just as she stopped in the middle of the street to take another breather. Lucky for her, the street was never busy with cars.

"Would you like some help with your shopping bags," I said pointing to the building across the street. "We live in the Annex over there. We'd be glad to help you get home."

She looked intently into our faces. Then she let go of the heavy shopping bags. "You girls look harmless enough, and redheads are, for the most part, decent people. I'm a redhead myself! Yes, please. I don't think I can go another step," admitted the gray-haired woman with a grateful smile.

Kathy and I each grabbed a shopping bag. My bag was full of cans and Kathy's had just as much food in hers, but they weren't too heavy for us. The woman talked and rested and talked and rested all the way to her apartment across the street from St. Stephen's. It took us half an hour at least to reach her first floor flat. If we were on roller skates, it would have taken one minute!

Bessie was her name. She lived with her

yellow-stripped tomcat, Amos. Amos was named after her first dead husband, who had died in the Great War, in 1918. Bessie was a fascinating talker, so by the time Kathy and I had put all of her groceries away in her kitchen pantry, we knew half her life story.

We learned that Bessie Hosnick had been married about every ten years, so she said. Each husband had died a terrible death. Two men died in different wars. Shortly after her first husband died in the war, Bessie became a dancer with the Ziegfeld Follies. The family horse bit another husband, and he died of blood poisoning. (I could relate to that!) The last husband past away from old age, he being much older and much richer than Bessie.

"Mr. Hosnick's grown children inherited all the cars, the house, and all of his money right after he passed. I'm left with just a few boxes of sentimental photos, clothes that don't fit me anymore, and my diamond ring. Presently, I'm just old, fat, ugly, sick,

AND poor! I don't even have my beautiful red hair anymore" she explained to us in great detail.

Poor Bessie! She was "fat, in poor health, lonely, and on welfare." I felt sorry for her and told Bessie that I could shop for her if she would let me. Bessie phoned Mum, and it was arranged that I could grocery shop for our new friend, Bessie. The sky was getting dark, so it was time for us to say our "goodbyes." Bessie got out her worn out change purse and pulled out a quarter for each of us. I tried to explain to Bessie that we couldn't take her money for doing a good deed. Bessie didn't insist on paying us. She smiled and put the two coins back in her purse. As we closed Bessie's front door behind us, Kathy cautioned me to not speak for her again!

Later I told Mary about Bessie. Although Mary was a widow, she was not poor. Mary did her own shopping. She always gave donations to the church and the Red Cross. And Mary was very generous whenever Kathy and I helped her out around her apartment or yard. She was a goodhearted person, but I worried that Mary wouldn't like it that Bessie and I were friends. I wondered if Mary would be all right with that friendship. Later that week, Mary and I went to visit Bessie. And they became more or less friends. Like I explained before, "Mary had a compassionate heart," and she helped Bessie too.

My first shopping trip for Bessie was a disaster. She spent most of her money on sockeye salmon for Amos. The salmon was for people; it had a price of 45¢ per can. On the other hand, salmon flavored canned cat food sold for 5¢ a can. You do the math. I was a smart shopper, always looking for bargains, but Bessie was a picky customer. I had to take back the sockeye salmon cat food and buy the people sockeye salmon. She wanted two-ply toilet paper, and it had to be a high priced name brand. The ketchup had to be Heinz. The butter had to be "real dairy." She had a rich taste on a poor woman's welfare check.

I never took money from Bessie for shopping. After about a month of weekly shopping, Bessie thought that we should go out to dinner on Fridays at the Italian Restaurant. Now in those days, Catholics never ate meat on Fridays. Bessie wasn't a Catholic, but she changed the day to Thursdays so that we could eat the meatballs with the spaghetti. I never ate spaghetti that wasn't made by my dad's hands, but she already changed the day. Therefore, I ate the spaghetti. Bessie taught me how to cut the pasta and not twist the spaghetti around my fork. She taught me restaurant manners and we had an excellent time.

Bessie talked, and I listened. Soon, I not only shopped for Bessie, but I cleaned her small apartment too. She squeezed into her upholstered easy chair like a queen. She ordered me around like a servant until the work was done. Housework will never be a good deed for me. I liked shopping, but housework was my limit. So when she offered me money, I took it! I got a quarter for all my hours of hard work.

*

It was during one of my cleaning days that Bessie showed me her mink outfit and her precious photographs. Under the bed, in a huge pink box, wrapped in tissue paper, was the most beautiful mink coat that I ever saw. Bessie explained to me that it was a full-length mink coat. Then she asked me to try on the coat as she took out her collection of faded black and white photographs from long ago. Soon after that Bessie dressed me in the hat, muff, and mink coat.

"You look just like me," Bessie sighed as she touched her thin gray hair.

Bessie showed me pictures of her when she was young. Forty years ago Bessie was an attractive and petite dancer. She showed me a picture of her with the last husband, Mr. Hosnick. They were bundled up in their matching mink coats in front of a black Lincoln Continental car. He was smiling for the camera, and she was holding on to his arm looking up at him with love in her hazel eyes. I learned a lot from Bessie about marriage, cats, the Ziegfeld Follies, and life. After our talk, we wrapped the mink outfit in the tissue paper and pushed the box back underneath her bed.

She wisely told me, "Once I had it all and then in a blink of the eye, things changed. I had to pick myself up and start with what I had left."

*

Sometimes Billy helped me shop for Bessie. Billy carried all of the shopping bags for me. Bessie didn't like Billy much because she always brought up the fact that, "You can't change the spots on a leopard."

Except I knew deep inside that Billy was a talented first-class kid with a heart of pure gold. I explained to her that, "Billy is a boy, not a leopard!"

*

I helped Bessie with her cleaning and shopping until my family moved away from the Burg when I was 16. Bessie was put in a "home" shortly after we moved away. I kept in touch with her through Mary. Mary visited Bessie often at the state home for the poor. The last time I saw Bessie was in 1971 when I came back to the Burg for a visit. She had both legs cut off at the knees because of her diabetes. Bessie described to me how she had to give her mink outfit to her sister, or the state could have taken it as payment for the hospital bills. I don't know what happened to her diamond ring.

Bessie revealed to me that Mary was now her best friend and was that Ok with me? We talked about my dad's death, pets, and the home. She warned me to, "Never get 'the sugar,' (diabetes) and never to get fat!" A week after I got back to California, Mary phoned and let me know that Bessie had passed away.

REMEMBER

Life changes like the seasons. And nothing lasts forever. Do the best that you can with what you have. And let the rest be in God's hands. Don't think, "They can wait. I'm too busy." Enjoy the people that you love now because they may be gone tomorrow.

OCTOBER days were cool.
The Buckeye tree's leaves changed to yellow.
We'd collect the brown buckeyes
When they dropped to the ground.
We would hollow out the insides
To make fairy baskets, or we would pound Holes
with screwdrivers and hammers so
We could make Indian necklaces.

When Our Mum was 42, she discovered that she was going to have another baby! It was just about that time that my oldest brother, Pete started to date a beautiful teenaged girl named Maureen. Pete wanted Mum to name the new baby, (if it was a girl), after his new girlfriend, but Mum told him, "No! I'm going to have a boy."

Again Mum compromised, "If I have another girl, maybe her middle name could be Maureen."

Well, what do you know? My adorable baby sister was born on October 31. Mum recalled that right after Kathy was born; Mum heard a faint musical sound, like a band playing. At first, she thought that the music was in her head. What Mum heard was the Halloween parade band, celebrating Halloween and the birth of our little baby sister, Kathleen Maureen Schumacher!

*

Trick or treating was always fun at the apartments. Mum dressed us up in our homemade costumes and around 5:00 the three of us walked out the door. We walked up the two flights of stairs to the fourth floor then we worked our way down to Mary's apartment. After Mary loaded us up on orange cookies wrapped in orange tissue paper and black ribbon, we would go out her front door to hit the street.

Our favorite place to trick or treat was on Franklin Ave. We'd hurry past our buckeye tree that grew tall in front of our second story porch and head for the Franklin house. Even now I don't know if the two men who lived in the Franklin house were brothers, or even if their last name was Franklin. Nevertheless, that's what Kathy and I called the two men who lived in the red brick house in the middle of the street. After we rang the doorbell on Halloween, the two Mr. Franklins opened their big wooden front door. It was in the backyard of the Franklin house that the Alley Rats dug most of our holes. They must have liked little kids digging in their yard because the Mr. Franklins didn't fence in their backyard like Mrs. Meyers had done.

Kathy would proudly say, "Today is my birthday! Trick or treat."

After Kathy had revealed that it was her birthday, both Mr. Franklins reached into their pockets and took out two brand new shiny quarters and gave the money to us. Next, the Mr. Franklins gave us extra candy. Trick or treating was over when our pillowcases were bursting at the seams. We'd race back to our apartment and divide up our candy. We would dump out the contents of our pillowcases on the red rug. We brought home apples, Mellow Cups, Clark Bars, homemade cookies, Milky Ways and tons penny candies. Mum took all the Hershey's bars because those chocolate bars were her favorites. Mum always admitted that she was a, "chocolate-holic." When everything settled down, we'd all sit down for supper and afterward have ice cream and cake for dessert.

*

Our Kathy was fortunate to have her birthday on October 31 because the next day was a holy day. So on November 1, we could sleep in after a night of gorging ourselves with our favorite kinds of sweets. In the morning, our family would walk the two blocks to St. James Church and attend Mass to celebrate All Saints Day.

*

Kathy and I went to the movies almost every Saturday. We could enjoy a whole bunch of cartoons plus a double feature for only a quarter. We called it the afternoon matinee. Most of the kids in the Burg started lining up outside the locked doors of the Roland Theater at about 11:30 a.m. just outside the entrance to the lobby of the Roland was a sizeable square-shaped opening in the sidewalk. The opening had an iron grate cover. All the patrons of the movies had to pass over the grating to get to the ticket booth. Some kids played with their money as they waited in line. They were the unfortunate people who would see some of their coins plunge and slip through the slits in the grate. Tearful children would tell the cashier at the ticket office that their quarters were lost and got in for free.

The line usually wrapped around the Mellon Bank at the end of the block, but at noon the doors opened, and the kids streamed in. If we were first inside the doors, Kathy and I would save some seats for our friends and then enjoy hours of entertainment in that magnificent old theater. Not only did we see cartoons and two movies, but also from time to time before the movies started, we saw magic shows, clowns, or a talent show. When the owner got on stage, we knew it was time for the door prizes—free candy or popcorn to the happy kids with the lucky ticket stubs. When the matinee was finally over around 4:30, and if we had some money left, we would go next door to Isaly's and get a skyscraper ice cream cone to eat on the way home.

*

Sundays in the Burg was "a day of rest." Everyone we knew went to Mass in the mornings, so most stores closed for the day. Isaly's and a few other Mom & Pop places stayed open on Sundays from noon until 5:00. Once in a while on a lazy Sunday afternoon, Kathy and I would gather our "fishing" supplies and try to fish out the lost quarters at the bottom of the metal grill outside the entrance of the Roland Theater. We needed at least seven feet of string, several small stones (fairy baskets worked best because of their tiny handles) and the most massive wad of sticky Double Bubble gum that could fit into my mouth for bait.

I'd tie a small stone to the string and then cover the stone with the immense glob of tacky bubble gum. Next, I would lay my face against the grate so that I could see down into the dark hole. I'd line up a slit in the grate with a lost quarter and push the bait through the narrow opening. After several attempts to line up the bait just above the quarter, I'd drop the sticky gum on top of the quarter. Then Kathy and I threw the heavier stones on top of the bait to make sure our treasure would stick to the bubblegum. Every so often we "caught a fish," but most times we just ended up with the striped imprint of the grate on our cheeks.

*

Some of my happiest memories from the past are about the Blooms. Mr. Bloom, the tailor, lived around the block from the Annex. He and his wife emigrated from Germany before World War II in the 1930s'. I don't know for sure because we didn't talk about the war, we talked about my brother Kenny.

One October afternoon when I dropped my dad's suits on the counter to be cleaned and pressed, I informed Mr. Bloom that Kenny had joined the army. A few months later, I reported to Mr. Bloom that Kenny was stationed in Germany. From that day on, no one in my family ever paid for dry cleaning again. Mr. Bloom considered Kenny a hometown hero. When Kenny came home on leave, we went to pay a visit to Mr. & Mrs. Bloom. Kenny wore his uniform with all of his merit emblems stitched on the front because I knew that Mr. Bloom would like to see him all dressed up. Mr. Bloom cried as he shook Kenny's hand, and told Kenny that he was a hero. They spoke in German and Kenny tried to explain that, "The war is over, and all I do is eat first-rate German sausages and wash them down with warm beer."

But, Mr. Bloom thought that Kenny was a hero because he helped the Jews in Germany. And that made the Blooms and I feel proud of my brother, Kenny.

*

Several years after that, Mrs. Bloom informed me that they were moving far away. "Everything must go, we are never coming back to the Burg," she confirmed with a smile.

She was happy, and I thought that the family was going back to Germany because now it was safe to be Jewish there. Or, even better for them, they were traveling to Israel, a nation created so that Jews could have their own homeland in the Middle East.

A few days later, I asked Mrs. Bloom if she would sell me the two elaborately golden framed paintings that hung in her dining room that I admired so much. One lithograph showed a petite girl peeking out of a partition spying on a small boy sitting on a chair. The matching lithograph showed a woman amusing herself by playing a harp while the two children listened close-by. I knew that Pete's beautiful new bride, Maureen, would love those pictures.

Everyone in our family loved Maureen, not only because of her beautiful smile when we visited her, but because everyone knew she was truly a good match for our brother, Pete. I wanted her to have something special from me so that she would know that I loved her like a sister.

I asked, "Mrs. Bloom, how much for the paintings? Pete's new bride would love them."

"One dollar each!" Mrs. Bloom replied with a grin.

I remember Pete telling me to negotiate, but one dollar each seemed like a fair price for old pictures dated 1901. Even though Pete paid the two dollars, those framed pictures came from me with all the love a 12-year-old girl could give her new sister.

Mr. Bloom tenderly wrapped each golden frame with brown butcher paper and twine as if they were bundles of shirts. I carried a package in each hand and gave the pictures to Maureen personally when I saw her. She loved them like I knew she would.

*

Pete and Maureen had the pair of lithographs displayed in the living room when I visited them on the July before Maureen passed away.

Maureen asked, "Hey, Jeanne, remember when you bought those pictures from Mr. Bloom?"

"I'll never forget it, Maureen," I answered. "Some things you never forget."

*

Recently divorced Alice moved into the fourth-floor apartment above the Sturks in late October. Alice had three blond-haired kids aged five, seven, and nine. Sally was the youngest. She dug large holes in the alley yards and buried her dolls in the holes. Many times I had to kick the dirt around and hope that a hand or a leg would pop up so I could uncover Susan's concealed Barbies. I introduced Sally to my friend Mary and soon it was Sally knocking on Mary's back door when the aroma of freshly baked sugar cookies rose through the fourth-floor transom. Mary loved visits from Sally. However, Mary didn't seem to like Martin and Robert because they were sneaky and devious. Since Robert was the middle child, he was the one who usually got caught because Martin blamed Robert for anything that Martin started.

A few weeks after the family moved in, Alice got a job as a waitress at the soda fountain down the street. So when I was thirteen years old, I started my babysitting career. I never looked after young babies, although I think the older kids are much more work. Alice could pay me 25 cents an hour if I watched her kids on Friday and Saturday nights. Since Dad lost his job, the extra babysitting money added to Bessie's cleaning money could help with my expenses. I liked to breakfast on a warm glazed donut on my walk to school every day. I also bought paper, school supplies, and several Gene Pitney records with my hard earned money.

*

My most memorable evening babysitting on the fourth floor was when we played hid-in-seek in the apartment. Most of the time the kids hid and I sought. As I counted to fifty, I heard the scrape of furniture and then silence. I discovered later that Martin and Sally moved a heavy dresser in front of the fire escape door so that Robert could not break out of the apartment. I found Martin first, near the dresser and he became the next finder.

Sally and I hid together in the front bedroom closet. Robert hid in the bathtub after he locked the bathroom door. Sally and I waited patiently among her mother's clothes. Martin searched out Robert and quickly discovered the locked door. Martin proceeded to find lighter fluid and saturate the hall rug in front of the locked bathroom door. Since it was too calm in the apartment, I realized something was up. Sally and I snuck out of the closet and caught Martin in the act of setting fire to the bathroom door!

I grabbed his hand before he struck the match. "I was going to smoke him out. He cheated," was Martin's reply.

Alice seemed shocked when I explained what had happened that night. However, I think Alice somehow knew that Martin was capable of other dark deeds.

Alice soon found a guy at the soda fountain and

started dating. He paid me 50 cents an hour when they went on dates. I was happy for Alice because she didn't seem sad anymore and she smiled more often. The guy was kind to the kids, but he was too nice to me. The guy started showing up an hour before Alice got off work just to talk to me. From then on, I made myself busy getting the kids ready for bed and read to them until Alice walked into the apartment. The guy sat on the sofa and stared at the television, but he seemed to be glancing at me.

One night Alice had to close the drug store, and she was going to be late getting home. So I had to put the kids to bed. The guy and I were alone in the dining room, and he was moving closer and closer to me. I was trying to avoid him, so we started going around and around the table. He was actually chasing me! Finally, I said that I was going home, and I left him to stay with the kids.

After that, whenever he showed up at the locked door, I opened the door and then I left. He stayed with the kids until Alice got home. The guy got the hint after that, and I continued to babysit for Alice to earn my extra money.

REMEMBER

Every day can be tomorrow's memories. Make the best with what you have, and stand up for yourself when you have to. Don't put today on pause. Don't waste a minute, an hour, or a day, because you can never go back and play it again.

NOVEMBER days were chilly and cloudy.
Everyone tried to predict
When the first snowfall of the year would begin.
The holidays were near,
So at night, Kathy and I
Would look at the Sears catalog
And cut out pictures to mail to St. Nick.

When the weather turned cold, we could always find our dad busy in the kitchen. He loved to cook and that suited Mum just fine. Some days Dad just threw leftovers that he discovered in the icebox into a big pot on the stove. Dad sprinkled salt and pepper, added some meat, and we had a healthy vegetable soup supper that would last for a few days. Neighbors could smell the aromas of Dad's concoctions whenever they opened their apartment doors.

*

Ever since I can remember, I did the grocery shopping for my family. Like I explained to you before, I even bought cigarettes for the priest, although, I never, in my life smoked one. Once in a while Mary and I would shop together, but most of the time I shopped alone.

*

Tony and his wife, Lena, lived above their grocery store with their kids. It was a "mom and pop" Italian establishment. I guess because Tony and Lena were the mom and pop to Tony Jr., my older brothers' friend. My family had a charge account at the grocery store. Whenever I bought deli meats, garden fresh tomatoes or Wonder bread from their store, I'd always say, "Charge it, Tony," and walk out the door.

One day Dad sent me to Tony's to buy the ingredients for his famous spaghetti sauce. "Jeanne, don't forget to get 2 pounds of Dagga sausage," Dad called out to me as I walked out the door.

I liked to go to Tony's Market because from time to time Tony would say, "Have a popsicle, on the house." "On the house," meant that I got some stuff for free. As usual, I walked in and let Tony know what we needed. Lena came out to say, "Hi, you wanta cupcake on the house?"

"Sure," I said with a hungry smile.

As I followed Lena over to the bakery section of their small store, I wanted to say something pleasant to her, since she was giving me the snowballs, "On the house." So I said, "My dad would never use any other sausage for his famous meat sauce. Your homemade Dagga sausage is the best!"

Well! Lena stopped in her tracks and turned around to face me. My smile faded as I looked up at her stern face. What did I do? Why was she mad at me? Lena forgot all about the cupcakes and hurried behind the meat counter. She took out the ground sausage and piled it on the waxed paper and weighed it. After that, Lena wrapped the 2 pounds of sausage in white butcher paper and marked the price with the fat black crayon that she always used.

"I'm gonna call your dad and tell him what you said," was all Lena told me as she handed me the wrapped sausage.

I slowly walked across the street thinking over and over again about what I had spoken to Lena to get her so angry with me. I couldn't for the life of me understand why Lena was so furious. When I got home, Mum took me aside and let me know that, 'Dagga' is not a kind word for an Italian person.

Mum explained to me that sometimes Dad uses "bad words." I felt ashamed of what I had repeated to Lena. So I rushed back to the store and with tears in my embarrassed brown eyes, I apologized to both Tony and Lena. I admitted to them that I was sorry and that I would go to confession and tell my sin to the priest. Which I did that very afternoon!

Lena gave me a warm hug, a Popsicle and a package of coconut snowballs. We were friends again. I never have spoken that word again or any other hurtful name about any race or culture of people.

*

When Thanksgiving came, Dad always started cooking the night before. He gathered everything that he needed to prepare the feast. Dad gave Kathy and me jobs to do, and it seemed that I was always "The Boss." Kathy and I helped him butter the bread and then cut the slices into cubes to bake for turkey stuffing. After we stuffed the turkey with sausage, sage, melted butter, bread cubes, and giblet broth, Dad stick the bird into the oven to cook all night. He'd get up several times during the evening so that he could baste the bird with ginger ale and butter. By the time our relatives arrived, the turkey was moist and ready to eat. Our Grandma Schumacher brought her licorice candy and buttermilk biscuits to share. Grandma Ryan baked the apple pies and made her famous ambrosia. Everyone brought something to share, but it was Dad's kitchen. After everyone was stuffed with delicious food and the kitchen was cleared, Dad placed the turkey leftovers and all of the fixings back in the roasting pan and took the pan to the porch. Most of the time we had frozen turkey leftovers by Friday morning.

*

There was always a pinochle game going on while Dad was cooking. My cousin, Jimmy Ryan taught me how to play pinochle when I was about six years old. He showed me how to arrange my cards and hold them. Since I was left-handed, Jimmy showed me how to flip the cards once the cards were in the correct order—red, black, red, black, with aces, tens, kings, queens, jacks and then the nines lined up in order. He taught me how to bid and meld. Jimmy Ryan was Pete's age, but he took the time to teach a little kid how to play cards. Once I learned how to play cards, I became the stand-in for anyone who had to go to the bathroom or leave the dining room table.

*

When I was six years old, Kenny left home to join the army, but our brother Pete still lived with us in the apartment. Pete was dating Maureen, going to college in the evenings, and he had a well-paying job at the Westinghouse plant not far from our home. Pete also bought a car from our Uncle Max. Pete was rich!

Whenever I needed money I'd go to my brother Pete. In Pete's closet, way in the back, hidden by a lot of dirty clothes was his personal bank. Pete put all of his change in a tall bongo drum. Kathy would help herself but I was going to become a nun, so I always asked Pete for spare change. I'd scratch Pete's back or shine his shoes. At other desperate times, I might ask my brother for money so that I could buy my lunch or get school supplies.

Here's a letter that I placed on Pete's desk one night when I was in the third grade:

Dear Pete,

If you have 45¢ would you Please give it to me Because I want to buy my lunch at school. And buy paper. But if you don't I could starve or faint. And get yelled at, at school because of no paper or lunch.

Your Loving Sister,
Jeanne
XXOOOXOO Please 45¢ I would do the same for you if you say, "Yes." But if you say, "No" or forget. I'll never talk to you. I'll get Puttenhead to spit at you and KiKi to sleep with you, and she has fleas.

I got the money the next morning. Pete always came through for me because he loves me and I love him. What other older brother would save a letter from his 8-year-old sister for over fifty years!

*

We didn't see much of Pete because he was so busy, but he was a marvelous older brother. He'd take the whole family to the country in the summers because he was the only one in our family that had a car. I can remember Kathy and I going to the drive-in with Maureen and Pete in the fall. Kathy and I would get the front seat so that we could see well and our brother and his date would sit in the back. Pete bought us hot dogs, cokes, Clark bars, and buttered popcorn to munch on during the double features plus cartoons.

*

There's only one time in my life that I remember Pete regretting his generously to me. One cold Saturday morning in November my lovable cat Puttenhead got hurt. I think he lost a fight in the alley because he looked all beat up in the face and chest. My cat's one eye was swollen shut. His eye looked like a gigantic marble was just waiting to burst out. Poor Puttenhead cried when I petted him.

He hardly moved and didn't eat or drink anything. He didn't use the sandbox. He just lay on my bed panting. I had to do something, so I phoned the Humane Society and desperately asked what I could do for my battered cat.

I was advised to bring my injured cat right over to the clinic. Since only Pete had a car, I begged Mum to ask him to take the cat to the vet. Now the reason I threatened Pete in my letter with the possibility of sleeping with KiKi and getting spit on by Puttenhead was that Pete hated cats—all cats, especially Puttenhead. Maybe it was because Puttenhead liked to carry half-dead mice into Pete's room and play with them under his bed while Pete tried to get some well-deserved sleep. Or it might have been that Pete had to help me with the heavy lid of the streetcar's sandbox when I needed more sand for Puttenhead's litter box. It could have been many reasons why Pete hated cats, but I just knew that he wouldn't like taking my precious cat to the vet.

Mum, Kathy and I begged Pete to drive Puttenhead to the clinic. "Get a box for the cat," Pete grumbled.

I put a towel in a box and then I carefully placed my sick cat inside. I slowly carried the box down the flight of steps.

"It's Ok Puttenhead, we're going to the doctor's, and you'll get well," I calmly whispered to him.

Reluctantly, Pete ran down the stairs to open the car doors for us. I gingerly sat down in the front seat with the box on my lap. Pete started up the engine with a whine and a bang. The noise startled my cat and Puttenhead leaped out of the box and crashed into the windshield. When his head bumped the window, Puttenhead's swollen eye opened up and out popped his eyeball! His eyeball was hanging about two inches below his eye— connected by the optic nerve cord. My poor kitty was a bloody mess. Secretions of pus and blood were splattered all over the dashboard and windshield of Pete's car.

Pete started screaming, "Get that stupid cat!" Except Pete's yelling frightened my sick kitty even more.

When a cat is scared, he starts to pee. I think my poor kitty was saving up a lot of pee because he sprayed from the windshield to the back window and everywhere in between, including Pete and me! Pete was still yelling when I grabbed my terrified kitty from the back seat and wrapped him in the towel. Somehow we made it to the clinic. The doctor couldn't save my cat, and he died. Worst of all for Pete, his car was ruined by that horrible cat urine stench. Pete tried everything to get rid of the stomach-turning stink inside his car, but nothing worked.

Finally, Pete gave his stinky car to Dad to drive. So thanks to my poor cat we now had a family car. I felt horrible about what happened to Puttenhead and Pete's car. After Dad passed away, Pete gave the car to Kathy. She loved that car and its unforgettable story. All these years I have tried to forget that awful event. Although from that day until today, fifty years later, whenever we are together all I have to say is, "Hey, Pete, remember the cat?" We all grin with the memory—Some of us more than others.

Our escapade with Puttenhead inspired the idea for a chapter in my second book in the Name Giver series; Mr. Grump goes to the Vet. Of course, in that story, the kitty lives happily ever after.

*

I'm sure that every family has a touch of sadness that creeps into the house at one time or other. Our family's sadness happened when I was eleven years old. One cold, cloudy November day, Dad came home early and informed us that he had lost his job at the furniture store. Mum went into her bedroom and cried, and Dad followed her. Kathy and I went into our room and sat on the bed together. Everyday Dad tried to get a job, but he was 57 years old and in 1962 that was too old for Dad to find a new job.

So Mum went back to nursing. She got a job right away at Columbia Hospital, the hospital where Kathy and I were born. The hospital was a few blocks from the apartment. Our Mother was a registered nurse, so she was responsible for the care of all the patients on her floor. Mum hated her responsibilities at the hospital because she was used to caring for two little girls, not fifty sick people, but she had to work because Dad couldn't find a job in sales. I prayed every night that things would go back to normal for our family, but our lives changed forever when Dad lost his job. Looking back now, I can see that God was lovingly watching over our family even though God didn't answer my plea exactly how I would have liked Him to.

*

At the time, I thought that some relatives got mad at Dad for losing his job. We didn't visit the McMuldrens anymore, and they never came to visit us. However, Kenny came through for us with steaks and fish. Kenny was a natural born salesman like our dad. He sold frozen meats to restaurants, part of his pay was in merchandise, and so we always had steak and breaded fish filets to eat.

Our Aunt Sis visited monthly and brought boxes full of good food. Kathy and I loved the jars of marshmallow cream that she bought for us. I think it was a topping for ice cream, but we used a spoon and couldn't get enough!

November has been a sad month for me. I have learned that when dreadful events take place in my life two things happen. I got stronger, with God's help and I learned who my true friends were.

REMEMBER

Study and learn from grown-ups. They have been around for a long time. Everyone has something to teach you—either good or bad. Pay attention to the people you like. Try to make their good traits your own.

DECEMBER had below-freezing winters

With ice storms and blizzards.

We would get up in the dark

And walk home from school at dusk.

No one would go out in the cold,

Unless we had to, we called it "Cabin Fever."

One of my fondest memories of my Catholic school education was when each student in my class received an empty cardboard milk carton after Mission Sunday. Our Sisters of Charity instructed us that we must save the "pagan babies" in foreign lands. Five dollars was what it cost to adopt a pagan baby. I gladly brought home my Holy Childhood money carton and began to fill the container with enough coins to adopt a child.

This one particular year I collected money from everyone in our apartment building. My goal was to adopt two baby girls. My friend Mary gave me five dollars right off the bat. The other neighbors gladly contributed coins after I explained to them what the pagan babies needed. I even asked George, the janitor if he wanted to contribute to the Christian charity. I had to explain to him what a pagan baby was because he seemed confused.

"Pagan babies are born in faraway lands. Catholic missionaries need the money to baptize the children and then buy seeds for their garden so the babies won't starve," I explained.

"Babies drink milk. What do the seeds do for the babies?" asked George, the janitor.

"The missionaries have to feed the parents and grandparents, so they stay inside the mission. Otherwise, the family might run away when it is time to go to daily Mass," I tried to explain.

George just shook his head. He didn't understand the concept of baptizing babies or for that matter, adopting "pagan" ones. He declared that he was a Southern Baptist.

"Oh," I whispered, not really knowing what that was supposed to mean. Then the salesperson in me made me say, "Well, I was thinking of adopting babies from Africa. I get to name them too. If you give me some of your extra coins, I promise I'll name a pagan baby after you." George gave me a dollar!

I thought long and hard about good Christian names. I knew that those lucky African children would have those names written in the book of life up in heaven. Finally, I selected the names of the fortunate babies that I saved. Of course, I named a boy "George" after the janitor. I also named the two girls, "Ann Theresa," after my favorite teacher and "Genevieve," after me. I secretly hoped that Genevieve would be born on January 3rd, just like me. At the end of the campaign, I received my three official adoption certificates. My certificates had a picture of the baby Jesus preaching to a couple of the pagan babies. George was so proud when I showed him the adoption papers. After that, he gave me a dollar for the pagan baby fund every December.

I haven't thought much about my pagan babies until I wanted to write this book. In hindsight, maybe I should have given my pagan babies strong African names. At the time, I did what I thought was best. I just hope my former pagan babies are happy knowing that a kid from the Burg worked relentlessly every December so that they could grow up safe with the missionaries in their country. And if you ever visit Africa and you hear someone call out to a very old woman, "Hey, Genevieve."

Do me a big favor and ask her if she was born on January 3rd in the 1960s'.

*

I was born with defected tonsils. Every winter my throat got inflamed, and I'd land in Mum's comforting bed for at least two weeks. Most of my Christmas vacations were spent in Dad and Mum's sick bed. Whenever anyone got a sore throat, Mum would make the Irish cure all—mustard plasters. She mixed a little bit of flour and prepared mustard with some water to make a paste. Next, Mum spread the mixture on a torn piece of sheet just like it was peanut butter. After that, she would wrap the mustard plaster in more pieces of torn cloth, so that it became a 4-inch square of comfort and relief. Finally, Mum placed the mustard plaster on my chest. I had to move it around because the mustard plaster got hot! The heat would help soothe my scratchy throat. Then I could spit out the tiny white pus balls that grew on my swollen tonsils.

For some reason doctors did not want to remove tonsils in the summertime (maybe because of the new polio cases that seemed to increase when the weather got hot), so until I was 11 years old, it seemed I was always sick around Christmas time.

When I was seven years old, Santa Claus came to the sick room to cheer me up. I was surprised when Santa opened the door. He gave me a record player with Elvis Presley's autograph on the lid. I also got three 45's (they were black vinyl records that you play at the 45 speed) with one of Elvis's songs on each side of the record. The more I played the records, the better I felt. I'll never forget when Santa came for that surprise visit. The magic of Santa Claus was very strong when I was seven.

*

For as long as I can remember, Mum never baked; so on Christmas Eve, Kathy and I bundled up. That means that we put on our leggings, boots, earmuffs, sweaters, scarves, gloves, and long winter coats on over our clothes so that we could go to Sherman's Bakery to buy Santa Claus his chocolate chip cookies. We liked to get waited on by Regina, the owner's daughter. Regina dated our cousin Jimmy, so she was always nice to us and gave us "cookies on the house." That means for free.

Every Christmas Eve Kathy and I would go to bed early because we knew that Santa had many long hours of work to perform at our house. As Kathy and I slept Santa delivered our Sears catalog presents and decorated the Christmas tree. That tree would stay up long after Christmas, long after my birthday and almost until the end of February. I guess Mum waited to see if Santa would come back to take down the tree, but he never did.

*

The best Christmas that Kathy and I ever had was when we got our fashion dolls from Kenny. Probably because we already knew what Kenny was giving us. Around my ninth Christmas, Kenny was discharged from the army. He got a part-time job at Gimbel's department store. Gimbel's was a very fancy department store in downtown Pittsburgh. Kenny bought everyone presents with his Gimbel's discount that year. It's just too bad he didn't hide the gifts in a better place.

One cold Sunday afternoon, a few weeks before Christmas, Kathy and I found two unwrapped boxes of fashion dolls behind Pete's bed. The dolls were beautiful. I liked the one with the short platinum hair. She wore a floor-length, black silky, evening gown with matching plastic high-heeled shoes. Her ears were pierced with dangling diamond earrings.

Kathy was left with the doll that had light brown curly hair. Her doll was dressed in a short black & white velvet dress with matching black flat shoes. Kathy's doll had a gorgeous diamond necklace and matching bracelet. The moment we pulled the dolls out of the box, Kathy wanted to give them a bath. We put our gifts back into their see-through boxes and snuck into the bathroom.

The minute that we went into the bathroom, there was no turning back. Although we knew we shouldn't be playing with the dolls now, we couldn't help it. Our dolls were so glamorous we couldn't help ourselves! I locked the door, and Kathy and I carefully undressed the fashion dolls. We turned on the water and filled the bathtub with bubbles. Then we stepped into the tub together, clothes and all (except for our shoes) with our dolls. Kathy grabbed the Break shampoo and washed her doll's hair. I was just about to snatch the bottle of shampoo from my sister's hands when Mum banged on the door. "What are you girls up too? Why is this door locked?"

Oh, we were caught! "I'm giving Kathy a bubble bath. We're almost done," I hollered.

Well, I didn't lie to my mother. We were taking a bath, and we were almost done. We drained the tub and rinsed the bubbles off the dolls. As we dried ourselves off, I noticed that Kathy's fashion doll's hair was shorter and a bit frizzier than before her bath. Kathy used a towel to dry her doll's hair, but the rubbing just made the hair tangled and more unmanageable. When Mum banged on the door the second time, we were almost done dressing the dolls. We pushed the dolls' feet first into the boxes and hid the boxes in the laundry basket. When I opened the bathroom door, Mum was out of sight. I motioned for Kathy to seize our dolls and put them back behind Pete's bed. I went to find Mum while Kathy put the bathroom back in order. Everything worked out fine. No one noticed that we had played with our fashion dolls before Christmas. That is until Christmas Day.

We opened all the other presents first. When the time came for Kathy and me to tear off the wrapping paper of Kenny's gifts, I looked him in the eye to see if he knew our little secret. All I noticed on his smiling face was love for his sisters and the pride that comes from knowing that his little sisters would love their fashion dolls. I opened my gift first. My doll was lovely with her beautiful platinum blond hair. I held her up for all to admire.

Then Kenny cried out "Where are her shoes?"

I looked in the box, but Marie Antoinette had lost her shoes—somewhere.

Of course, the biggest shock to Kenny was when Kathy opened her present. Her fashion-model doll's hair was one big frizz ball. The poor doll had no necklace or bracelet, no shoes, and no underwear! All that Kenny could say was, "What happened to her?"

"I den' know," Kathy whispered as she smiled in her best innocent expression.

We loved our fashion dolls and lovingly carried them to St. James Church with us later on that day. Kenny had guessed that we found his gifts before Christmas because the next year we searched the whole apartment, but my sister and I didn't find anything that we could put in a bubble bath.

*

A few years after Dad lost his job and Pete and Kenny had moved out, our Uncle Leo moved in with us. He stayed with us when Mum worked at the hospital, and Dad looked for a job at other furniture stores. Uncle Leo slept on the couch in the front room at night. He rolled his cigarettes, which means that he made his own cigarettes with paper and tobacco. He smoked and smoked. Sometimes Uncle Leo had two cigarettes lit at a time, one in his mouth and one waiting its turn in the ashtray.

After Kenny got a divorce, he would stay in his old room too. Then Kathy and I slept together in Pete's old room. When our parents, Uncle Leo, and Kenny were in the house together, our house was like a smokehouse.

It was during this time of the year that a terrifying series of events took place at the Annex. The first time it happened I woke up in the middle of the night and knew something dreadful was happening. Everyone in our apartment was asleep. Kathy was sound asleep beside me, so I poked her and asked, "Do you smell wood burning?"

I got up and switched on the bedroom light. My bedroom was full of a gray haze of smoke! I looked up at the transom above the door that led out into the building's hallway and saw black smoke pushing its way into the small crevice surrounding the window and its frame. I opened my bedroom door and ran to my parent's room across the hall. Dad rushed to the front door and felt the warm heat trying to pass through the wooden door. We all turned around and headed for the fire escape. A bleary-eyed Uncle Leo met us in the hallway. Kenny woke up when we all rushed into his old room to escape through the fire escape door in Kathy's bedroom. We grabbed some blankets and hurried down the iron stairs, shouting "Fire! Fire!"

When we were safe in Mary's yard, we could see the flames shooting out of the basement windows. Just as the smoke and flames curled up into the cold night air, many things happened at once. Uncle Leo turned around and ran up the fire escape stairs back into our smoky apartment. Then Alice and her children cried out for help from their fourth-floor apartment porch.

"Oh, no!" I cried out. "Their fire escape door is blocked by a massive dresser."

Kenny turned around and charged up the iron steps three at a time. All of us watched him fly up to the fourth floor in his blue jeans and bare feet. Next, he jumped on to the black railing and climbed inside a bedroom window in Alice's smoke-filled apartment. Seconds later he pushed open the fire door, and Alice and her two boys ran to the security of the yard below. As Kenny hurried down the fire escape with Sally in his arms, he met up with Uncle Leo. Our uncle had rushed into the burning apartment building to rescue his cigarette producing materials! Everyone got out in time, and no one was hurt.

Someone had set fire to the storage lockers in one of the laundry rooms in the basement. That long night was the first of many small fires that frightened the Alley Rats. For the next few months, we'd have to rush out onto the fire escape and met the residents in the yard below. Everyone had the shadowy dark smoke marks below our noses and the look of dread on our faces.

"When will these fires stop?" We all asked each other.

In the spring, the chapel below St. James Church caught fire, and everyone found out which Alley Rat was responsible for the winter nightmares. Although I guessed it could have been Martin, I was relieved to learn that the firebug was not the little boy that I babysat on the weekends.

*

Not every day was filled with the excitement of

Christmas and scary basement fires. Most days in the winter were boring, especially as I got older. One thing that bothered me was the flipping TV. As long as I could remember, our black & white television set's horizontal hold was on the fritz. For that reason, the picture would flip about every five seconds. If we timed it just right and blinked our eyes every five seconds we were not distracted but... "It was nerve-racking," as Mum used to say.

As a result of years of blinking my eyes, I was determined to fix the flipping television myself. In the 1960s', all electronic equipment including our television set had a multitude of glass tubes in the back. I knew about these tubes because at Botzer's Drug Store there was a free Tube Tester Machine. I decided to test every tube in the back of our broken television!

I unplugged the electrical cord of the annoying television and unfastened the screws on the cardboard backing. When I removed the back cover, I saw dozens of glass tubes in all shapes and sizes. Although most of the glass tubes were clear glass, some looked like a burned out light bulb, kind of smoky inside. I made a map of the location of each burned out tube on grid paper and began removing three tubes at a time. I put the tubes in my coat pocket and after bundling up in all my winter gear; I took off to test the tubes at the drug store.

When I got to Blotzer's I patiently began testing each tube. I found out that at the bottom of each rounded end, right above the prongs was a letter and some numbers of that individual tube. The free tube tester machine had easy directions, just like the poster explained, "As easy as 1,2,3,4."

#1 find the letter at the bottom of the tube.

#2 locate the corresponding letter and plug the tube into the square on the testing machine.

#3 press black test button.

#4 Green light means Ok. Red light means burned out. Yellow light means replace.

After four hours of pulling out tubes, marking down the location, coat on, testing, and retesting, coat off, and putting tubes back in place. I was finished! I bought two dollars and fifty-nine cents worth of tubes with my babysitting money. I plugged the new tubes inside the television, tested the picture, which was perfect—even brighter than before AND, not a flip to be seen. Then I waited. I didn't tell anyone that I had fixed the television.

I wanted it to be a surprise for my family, although the surprise was on me. Even though everyone sat down to watch The Perry Mason Show that evening, no one noticed that the television set was fixed. When Perry Mason, the world famous attorney, was in the courtroom and no one noticed that he didn't do backflips any more, I decided that I wouldn't say a word, no matter how long it took for them to notice. A few days later Pete and my cousin, Jimmy Ryan, came over with some Christmas gifts for the family.

The moment Jimmy stepped into the living room, he cried out "I can't believe it! You finally got the flipping television set fixed!"

"What?" Uttered Dad.

"Well, I'll be!" Declared Mum.

"You're right, son!" Stated Uncle Leo.

Kathy giggled. Pete did a double take, between Jimmy and our TV. I just sat there on the worn-out green Chesterfield with my arms folded across my chest, "Finally!" I grinned.

REMEMBER

Christmas is for Jesus and little kids. Never forget why He was born. Celebrate your love of the season by doing good deeds. Be good to one another, today and every day of the year. Keep the spirit of Christmas alive in your heart, always.

In the summer of 1967, we had to move out of the Annex. The owners sold the two apartment buildings, and the new owners were tearing them down to build modern apartments. We were the last family to move out after school let out in June.

Some nights as I was stretched out in my bed, the quiet of the vacant building overwhelmed me. Just about the time that I was drifting off to sleep, if I really listened very hard, I could hear the ghost of a teenaged boy, singing in the Franklin Tunnel late into the night. He sang the songs of my youth.

Months turn into years just as quickly as these pages of my memories turned into a story. I'll always remember parts of those ordinary days because each month shaped me into the person that I am today.

CHRISTMAS TIME

OUR DAD

PETE, MAUREEN, KATHY, & I OFF TO THE DRIVE-IN.

5TH GRADE ST. JAMES

KATHY & ME

GRANDMA & PUP-PUP RYAN

THE COLONIAL AND THE ANNEX WHEN THEY WERE BUILT

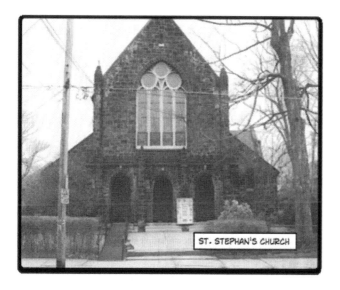

ST. STEPHAN'S CHURCH

PUP-PUP AND US

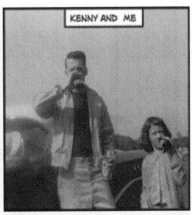

KENNY AND ME

KATHY & I

GRANDMA SCHUMACHER AND MY 1ST COUSINS

ME, DAVID, & MARYANN

THE DAY WE MOVED OUT OF THE ANNEX

ABOUT THE AUTHOR

G. m. Staley lived in the Burg for 16 years. She has wonderful memories of her childhood. Maybe she just remembers the good times, but she was loved and protected by the people who walked into her young life. Every event has shaped her life in some way for the best. AND many lessons were learned from the people who shared her world in the Burg. Her old apartment building, The Annex is the setting for the first six books in the Name Giver series.

Mrs. Staley is also the creator of the Name Giver series of stories about a kitten's first year of life in search of her Name Giver & THE ADVENTURES OF MASON THE BLUE MOUSE. She lives in CA with her husband and many of the animals mentioned in her books. Visit G. m. Staley on her Facebook page and let her know how much you enjoyed her books.